248.4
E46

Ellingsen, Mark

Sin bravely

JUN 1 0 2009

SIN
Bravely

MARK ELLINGSEN

SIN *Bravely*

A JOYFUL ALTERNATIVE
TO A
PURPOSE-DRIVEN LIFE

continuum

NEW YORK • LONDON

2009

The Continuum International Publishing Group Inc.
80 Maiden Lane, New York, NY 10038

The Continuum International Publishing Group Ltd
The Tower Building, 11 York Road, London SE1 7NX

www.continuumbooks.com

Copyright © 2009 by Mark Ellingsen

All rights reserved. No part of this book may be reproduced, stored
in a retrieval system, or transmitted, in any form or by any means,
electronic, mechanical, photocopying, recording, or otherwise,
without the written permission of the publishers.

Library of Congress Cataloging-in-Publication Data

Ellingsen, Mark, 1949–
  Sin bravely : a joyful alternative to a purpose-driven life / Mark
Ellingsen.
    p. cm.
  Includes bibliographical references.
  ISBN-13: 978-0-8264-2964-3 (pbk. : alk. paper)
  ISBN-10: 0-8264-2964-5 (pbk. : alk. paper) 1. Sin—Christianity.
2. Warren, Richard, 1954– Purpose-driven life. 3. Christian life.
4. Christianity—United States. I. Title.

  BT715.E45 2009
  248.4—dc22

                                                2008045476

Printed in the United States of America

9780826429407

TO BETSEY

My life-long companion in brave sinning

CONTENTS

PREFACE

I've tried to make this book an exercise in brave sinning, since I am writing about the subject. It certainly is an audacious undertaking, and I am most aware of its flaws (especially the flaws of its author). I mean, what could be more audacious than to put before educated readers the main arguments of papers written nearly forty years ago during one's undergraduate senior year? Sure, since that time I've learned a lot about Neurobiology and its exciting findings pertaining to the workings of the human brain. I have studied a lot more of Martin Luther's writings than I had when I was twenty. But certain feelings and passions of that sixties-era college student have not changed much.

How well I remember my first exposure to the writings of Martin Luther and his concept of brave sinning. Wow! Though reared Lutheran, I had not been well taught about the profound and joyful Word of God's unconditional forgiveness and love. This may be an even bigger problem within American Lutheranism (and in American Christianity) today, as Luther's heritage is more and more forgotten even in the church that bears his name. As for Luther's idea that the best a Christian can do is sin bravely—that talk about piety and striving for perfection portrays realities impossible to achieve and is in fact legalism, and so we can chill out and enjoy our service to God and our neighbors—that liberating idea made Christianity really come alive for me. I began to realize for the first time that being a Christian was a rebellious lifestyle. It could be cool to be Christian—even antiestablishment!

But alas, though most Religion scholars have heard of this phrase (and there is even a website devoted to brave sinning), the concept is not widely disseminated in undergraduate Religion programs, in seminaries, or in graduate schools. As a result, American Christianity remains duty-oriented and the concept of "sinning bravely" is largely unknown in the pews—even among Lutheran laity. These observations saddened me forty years ago; they sadden and even anger me today. I want the Church to take God's unconditional grace more seriously and have fun doing it. That's the sense in which this book is just an amalgam of my undergraduate theological meanderings. I'm still the same old sinful gracefreak I was then.

All the theological movements with broad impact today are the antithesis of a vision of brave sinning. They succeed, I think, because they are creative, even sometimes thoughtful versions of American Christianity's preoccupation with duty-oriented (almost Puritan) versions of the faith. Americans, indeed all human beings, like to do for themselves, even in religion. Of the theological strands having the broadest impact in America today, in the tradition of Billy Graham, Rick Warren's Purpose-Driven model is probably the best. That's why I wanted to focus on a study of his core theological commitments. And since the Prosperity Gospel is also having a significant impact on American religious life today, I thought I needed to consider it along with Warren, to point out precisely why they will not make you as happy and free as a life of brave sinning can.

My bold aim, marred as it is by this author's ego, is to present Luther's joyful, rebellious vision to scholars, the Church, and even to the public—and to argue for what a difference it might make. As I write these words I am sensing with pleasure some of the passions, excitement, and dreams of that twenty-year-old undergraduate to whom I introduced you. That's another one of the reasons this book is an exercise in brave sinning. I only hope that these feeble words become vehicles for conveying these passions and joy to you.

I also hope it will be obvious that these passions and my excitement about viewing the Christian life as a life of brave sinning have not cooled over the years. But my first exposure to the concept at Gettysburg College transpired so long ago that none of my instructors are left to thank who introduced me to the insight, save a beloved ninety-year-old, a mentor to many, Harold Dunkelberger. Thus thank-yous for this book will be few, save to Martin Luther himself. Of the few recent Luther scholars who have tried to get the Church and academy to appreciate Luther's concept, Eric Gritsch was probably the most effective. Though I never sat in his classroom, I am pleased to consider myself his student, at least informally. I have also benefited much from the advice of my careful and talented editor Burke Gerstenschläger in the development of this book.

But the most crucial person to credit, though, especially through lots of conversations about religion and the workings of the human mind—and even more so by sinning bravely together over thirty-seven years—is my best friend and confidante Betsey Shaw Ellingsen. She's also been the first editor for this and all fourteen of my other books. How many times over the years, while doing the usual things spouses do for each other, have we confessed to each other how both of us were getting lots of pleasure out of the relationship, or spent time marveling about how extraordinary it is that an undergraduate native New Englander and an immigrant's kid from Brooklyn studying at an Ivy League graduate institution met on a Catholic campus and were mutually attracted? Maybe those are some of the reasons why our own life together seems to have gone so fast and been so much fun.

Introduction

Why It's More Fun to Be
Brave in Your Sinning

There is little doubt in the minds of most observers that Rick Warren has become the most influential American Evangelical, if not the most influential Christian pastor in America.[1]

Author of the close to 30 million best-seller *The Purpose Driven Life* (the best-selling hardback in American history) and before that a million-seller for church leaders, translated into over twenty languages, *The Purpose Driven Church*, Warren is Founding Pastor of one of America's largest congregations, Saddleback Valley Community Church, in Lake Forest, California. He presides there over a congregation of 15,000 members and an additional 5,000 visitors weekly, with 400 paid staff and a $19 million budget. His influence goes far beyond his publications. Movie moguls like Mel Gibson have sought his advice on religious themes in their films, the White House sought his advice on how to observe the first anniversary of 9/11, he convened an important forum involving the major candidates in the 2008 Presidential elections, and was invited to assume a leadership role in the Obama inauguration ceremonies.

Warren's influence has not been the result of a media ministry like some of America's most well-known megachurch pastors. He does not broadcast his sermons on TV. His greatest influence stems from the network of pastors who have used his books, implementing them in more than 10,000 congregational programs or using them in small-group studies on purpose-driven living or purpose-driven church life. As long ago as early 2004, nearly 300,000 ministers from all 50 states and 120 nations had participated in Warren's pastor-training seminars and Internet classes.

To date, critical examination of the ministry of this son of a Northern California Baptist minister, who left home to be trained at Southwestern Baptist Theological Seminary in Fort Worth, Texas, has focused on his marketing techniques. At least some of these assessments have been critical, contending that he has appealed to American business notions that size equals success, that salvation and growth are conflated.[2] However, no one has critically examined Warren's conception of purpose and the purpose-driven life which is so crucial to his ministry and the impact he is having throughout America and worldwide. This book will alert Americans and international readers of Warren's work that his vision will not provide all it promises, that it will not give Christians and American society what they need.

I come not to bury Warren, but to praise him—sort of. There is much to be admired in the way in which Rick Warren has lived his life and conducted his ministry. I even find a lot to admire in his theological convictions. Although regrettably he shares some commonalities with proponents of the Prosperity Gospel (the belief that God will materially bless his followers who have the right frame of mind), analysis in this book will make clear that Warren and these preachers like Joel Osteen, Kenneth Copeland, Bruce Wilkinson (who does not want to be seen as advocating the Prosperity Gospel vision, while praying for increased business), and Creflo Dollar should not be confused. Warren's endeavor to offer an alternative to the self-seeking cultural narcissism that characterizes much American life is a commendable project.[3] But unfortunately, as my book will demonstrate, this highly influential megachurch leader has not delivered entirely on his aims.

The reasons for Warren's success in our context are in fact related to the shortcomings of his purpose-driven vision of life. His stress on purpose nicely links with the dominant emphases of the main strands of American religiosity—a sort of semi-secularized Puritanism tinged with heavy doses of Revivalism. I will elaborate in this volume on some points I've made in a number of my previous books.

The dominance of Reformed (especially Puritan) thought on the American religious psyche is increasingly recognized among scholars.[4] One consequence of this impact on America has been the propensity it has created among Americans to understand as virtually synonymous being religious, being a good citizen, and having a strong work ethic that includes individual morality. In part, the success of Warren's purpose-driven message is that it links up with this duty-oriented conception of faith and life. But as I will demonstrate especially in the first two chapters, the consequence of all this is that Warren unwittingly confirms American society's current preoccupation with the self. The result is that the vision of faith he proposes can result in a life of guilt and sense of inadequacy. It also fails effectively to challenge contemporary American society's business mania and Narcissism.

We need a countercultural alternative to the characteristic vision of American religion. The new (it's really an ancient) vision I'm proposing for America's consideration can make us happy. It could also change the character of American life. Instead of a life *driven* by purpose, let's have more fun. A life of *brave sinning* is the way to go to get happiness and contentment. Brave sinners are a lot more dependent on God than those driven by purpose. Brave sinners are also more likely to subvert the insalubrious trends in contemporary society I've just noted; they could change American life.

Although I will elaborate in detail on the concept of brave sinning in chapters 3 and 4, I had better say something about what it entails right here, or you may incorrectly get the impression that I am advocating sheer wild living (a "do your own thing" lifestyle) as a rival to Warren's call for purpose. No, the concept of brave sinning has roots dating back to St. Paul, the early African theologian St. Augustine, and especially to the great sixteenth-century Reformer Martin Luther who elaborated their doctrine of original sin in order to emphasize our dependence on grace and the love of God. Once you concede, with an Augustinian reading of Paul (see Romans 7:14–23), that we can never avoid sinning in anything we do, then it follows that even the actions of redeemed Christians will be marred by sin.[5] What you do with this insight is what makes the difference between being a brave sinner or a "pretended" and "cowardly sinner."[6]

The difference between brave sinning and pretended sinning is not trivial. Pretended and cowardly sinners do not own up to their sinfulness. They are people committed to living "virtuously," dare we say with purpose. Sure they face temptations, but they also think that by strength of character they can avoid sin. The pressure is on pretended sinners to be good, because in their own minds they are not really sinners. You spend a lot of time worrying about yourself when you are a pretended sinner. This outlook on life is pretty much the American way—at least it is the ideal. In the first chapter we'll see how Rick Warren's purpose-driven way of life resonates with many Americans so well precisely because it plucks these strings.

Another version of pretended and cowardly sinning is to concede that you might be a sinner, but so what? Being a pretended sinner makes you self-concerned. But self-concern can easily become an obsession, until caring about yourself becomes more important than being good in the eyes of your community. This dynamic pretty well explains what has happened in American and in Western society in the past century (at least since World War II here in the U.S.). Influenced both by developments in high culture as well as by the media and pop culture, and now receiving spiritual blessings from proponents of Prosperity

Gospel, the capitalist preoccupation with self-interest has been transformed into a kind of social narcissism—an excessive preoccupation with one's pleasure to the extent that the self overrides all boundaries such that other people, relationships, institutions, values, and life's tasks become nothing more than vehicles for the individual's gratification.

Brave sinners confess that they are not less caught up in egocentricity than Narcissists and other proponents of the "do what feels good" lifestyle. But brave sinners are bold enough to say no to this sort of lifestyle. They also dare to try to find ways of saying no to their self-preoccupations. Brave sinners boldly look for projects and values bigger than they are. They bravely subordinate their desires for instant gratification to helping people, supporting institutions, or remaining faithful to good values and commitments. But they also realize and confess that all these apparently "good" deeds are produced by egocentric drives, and so are sins, that if any good comes out of such actions it is truly a miracle (transpiring only because God made something good out of them). Brave sinning makes you more God-centered, more inclined to give God all the credit for any and all good.

In the last two chapters I will explore in more detail why the life of brave sinning makes for more happiness and how the nurturing of such a lifestyle in the church could change America, change the West. We'll examine the specifics of recent neurobiological research which bears out my (and Martin Luther's) claim that selfishness tinges the most beautiful of all human activities, but that brave sinners are happier, have more fun. It seems that when human beings forget themselves, focus on God and on bigger, meaningful projects, or on other people more than they do themselves, the back part of the brain which functions to orient us in space and time (the parietal lobe) becomes less active. Instead, a portion of the front part of the brain goes into overdrive. This activated part of the brain (the frontal lobe, especially the outer layer of gray matter on its left side, the prefrontal cortex) is then bathed in pleasurable brain chemicals that produce sensations of contentment and happiness. "Other-directed" people experience more happiness and pleasure without even trying, it seems, than those preoccupied with pleasure. And related to the experience of such happiness, body mechanisms are touched off which can improve health and (as I'll demonstrate in a future book sometime) even retard the aging process.

Just as this book went to press, the leading Neurobiological researcher of religious experiences, Andrew Newberg, was about to have a new volume released (co-authored with Mark Waldman), *How God Changes Your Brain.* But pre-publication information indicates that it does not substantially alter the findings I report of research in the field conducted by him and other colleagues. Newberg's new book also does not provide a distinctly Christian guide for stimulating the beneficial brain mechanisms like my volume does.

The Christian concept of brave sinning provides a vision that could change our way of life in the West. Especially in America, with our preoccupation about economic advancement and the need to be on the job 24/7 (to heck with vacations), the life of brave sinning will undermine this sort of idolatry, our present incentives to do business only with short-term gain in view, and our tendency to demonize those not "making it" (i.e., the poor). To be sure, brave sinners will put in a good day at the office. But they also know that what happens on the job, especially how it impacts their careers, is ultimately not that important. Since all that happens in life is marred by sin, it follows that nothing is going to be perfect, not even our relationships. Life will be a lot better when we get over taking everything so seriously, especially the things that pertain to our own aims and self-image.

Brave sinners who are having fun in life tend to see life and the projects in which they are involved as joyful play. Aware of their fallibility, of their unworthiness, brave sinners are also cognizant that whatever good they have accomplished or have enjoyed in life is not really their doing, that they do not really deserve these goods or the praise and power bestowed on them. This in turn entails an awareness that those who have not achieved, the poor and disenfranchised, are no less worthy of the goods others have. Brave sinners do not demonize the poor, as they recognize that but for the grace of God it could be them. Coupled with the other-directedness of brave sinning, an America populated by brave sinners is likely to be a more caring, friendly place for the immigrant and the disadvantaged. Prosperity and success are not "measures of the man," not signs of faith, for brave sinners. Brave sinning, we will discover, can change American life.

This may be an academic book, but that doesn't mean it can't be practical. Consequently in the conclusion I will also consider some practical ways in which the life of brave sinning might be facilitated and made concrete in your life. Once you're clear on the nature of Sin, understand it as a daily reality in your life, and fully recognize your dependence on God in every aspect of life, you're likely to become grateful, yearn for a better world and your part in it, organize life around projects that are bigger than you are, and have more fun. Purpose takes care of itself when you are brave in your sinning.

Reflecting on the shape of this alternative way of life jumps the gun, gets us thinking about a new way to live, a new era. We first need to look at the old order in which you and I presently find ourselves to be residing. This is where our study of what Rick Warren and his impact teaches us about our present religious and social situation is essential for setting the stage for examining my Pauline-Lutheran alternative. It is to the tasks of understanding Warren's vision and our context that we now turn.

Rick Warren and
American Christianity
What's Good and What's Bad

Rick Warren is on the right track in many ways. Political and business consultants have observed how his ministry embodies all the things necessary to connect with Americans today. He has established and maintained a "Gut Values Connection" with the people, offering both a sense of community and a higher purpose in life. He also projects Authenticity, is Adaptable in his ministry, has practiced Life Targeting of his audiences through Niche Marketing, Communicated Effectively and Professionally, and Authorized Navigators (small-group leaders who exercise significant influence over the group).[1] He has clearly learned lessons from his administrative mentor, management consultant Peter Drucker.

As will become obvious in our subsequent analysis, Warren is correct in reading contemporary American society as having so glorified the individual over the community that we have created a generation of very lonely people.[2] His ministry strategy, typical of other successful megachurch pastors, of building a church with enough small groups for everybody to feel at home and find friends offers lonely Americans communities for which they yearn.

Each of these small groups has leaders who function as "Navigators," exerting significant word-of-mouth influence over the members of the group by helping them to navigate the perils of modern living. Business-management gurus and political consultants agree that such Navigators are crucial for successfully marketing products in this post–computer revolution age.[3]

Americans, it seems, are also yearning for meaning and purpose in life. Warren's emphasis on purpose-driven living applies directly to this search and is crucial to his success. I will devote most of my attention to this emphasis. But the messenger and the way the message has been packaged also contribute to this influential megachurch pastor's accomplishment.

Americans today, living in an age of cynicism and irony as we do, desire authenticity in their leaders. Rick Warren is simply a nice, regular guy, who doesn't have a big ego and doesn't crave attention. He also seems to be "Mr. Clean" (a man with no personal or financial skeletons in his closet), much after the fashion of Billy Graham, his model in ministry.

Adaptability and niche marketing done professionally are the earmarks of Warren's Saddleback Church. Because of its size and impressive resources, the congregation has offered numerous engaging ministries and different forms of worship, each geared to different constituencies/markets. Of course offering many options is the sine qua non for a successful operation that will appeal to a generation of Americans used to choices in how they live and are entertained. The Internet, cable television, a flexible job market, and the sexual revolution have taught us to expect to be offered options (even within our religion).

Saddleback's rich variety of programs is marketed in most attractive ways, including sophisticated use of computer technology. From the founding of Saddleback as a mission congregation, Warren has had a distinct target audience (market) in mind

(Baby-Boomer, unchurched, white-collar couples), and the ministry has been marketed and developed to attract that audience. This sort of niche marketing is the way to grow a business or get elected within today's ethos of customization.

If Rick Warren's ministry was not as skilled in its marketing and diverse in its programming, he would probably not have the influence he does today. But for the most part thus far we have been attending to the media he uses, not the message. When we get clear on his message (his stress on purpose) we can also account for his success in other ways. We will observe intriguing similarities between his emphases and the dominant emphases of American Christianity. These similarities explain why so much of what Warren teaches resonates with the majority of American Christians. His purpose-driven model is speaking their language (or at least offers a model of Christianity that seems to offer a vision of what they intuitively think life should be like).

RICK WARREN ON PURPOSE
IN OUR NARCISSIST ETHOS

In addition to the other wise and commendable strategies of his ministry and his personhood, Rick Warren is on the right track with regard to his starting point for his theological reflections. He begins his best-selling book *The Purpose Driven Life* in such a promising fashion, contending that "It's not about you," and that "[t]he purpose of life is far greater than your own personal fulfillment, your peace of mind, or even your happiness." Rather, he contends, we must begin with God.[4] He is also absolutely correct in my judgment when he elaborates on this point by maintaining that focusing on our dreams, ambitions, and feelings is a dead end. Our own agendas will not reveal God's purpose.[5]

I have suggested the primary reason for Warren's theological predispositions at this point. Recall his contention that Westerners have so glorified the individual over community as to create a modern culture of Narcissism.[6] Again his diagnoses seem on target.

Almost thirty years ago, the historian and eminent social commentator Christopher Lasch categorized American life as Narcissistic in character. Borrowing the term from a pathological disorder identified in the field of clinical psychology, Lasch contended that many Americans and the media's vision of social life had become so caught up with purely personal preoccupations like self-fulfillment as to blur the boundaries between self and world, so that people and life's task lost their own independent value, becoming nothing more than vehicles for the individual's gratification.[7] Such a blurring of boundaries effectively isolates many Americans from others, from their institutions, and even from a concern about the future or the past. All that matters is pleasure in the moment. But because of such isolation of the individual, the self is empty. Seeking madly to fill this void, American Narcissists try to gain celebrity (the affirmation of others), even if it is without achievement, or to gain affirmation through therapy. These dynamics help explain the widespread popularization of a "soft," optimistic version of Sigmund Freud's insights in American society since World War II.

A lot of data supports Lasch's analysis (and so Warren's assessment of our context as well). The perdurance of a therapeutic ethos that undergirds our social Narcissism is still clearly in place. Crime and our problems continue to be cast in the therapeutic jargon of being "dysfunctional." Unruly or mischievous school children are excused as having Attention Deficit Disorder (ADD). People continue to be encouraged to "get in touch with their feelings," "meet their needs," and find or nurture self-esteem. The need to avoid codependency is frequently invoked as justification for breaking commitments. Much antisocial behavior today is interpreted as an addiction, such as the latest malady, Computer Addiction. The popularity of Dr. Phil McGraw and the fact that 23 percent of the Baby Boom generation as well as 18 percent of women and 13 percent of men in the total population have reportedly received psychological counseling further testifies to the continuing impact of the therapeutic ethos on American life.[8]

Other modern trends support the continuing validity of Lasch's diagnosis of the Narcissism in American society. The Narcissist craves celebrity and is attracted to celebrities. Thus we make celebrities our heroes in twenty-first-century America. This helps explain the Reagan and Schwarzenegger phenomena in American politics. Celebrity magazines sell widely. Modern computer technology feeds this passion both here and in Western Europe. It has provided ordinary Americans with the hope, if not the opportunity, to become celebrities themselves, accounting for the stunning popularity of *American Idol*. And then there is the way computers allow us to self-publish books or have our lives broadcast on screen worldwide on YouTube. This infatuation for celebrity is also part of the business ethos. Self-promotion, building an image as a winner, is sometimes more important to your career than accomplishments.

The persistence of the isolated individualism associated with the Narcissism described by Lasch and Warren in the twenty-first century is easy to document. A 2004 survey revealed that 25 percent of Americans have no one in whom they feel they can confide. While in 1985, the majority of Americans had three people in whom to confide, by 2004 that number had dropped to two. The percentage of people who only confide in family increased from 57 percent to 80 percent. In Europe, Narcissism has nurtured a new tribalism contesting traditional social constraints and the European union movment.[9]

Having forfeited an appreciation of historical perspective, Narcissists crave instant gratification and sometimes seek it through the accumulation of goods and sexual adventures. There is plenty of statistical and poll evidence that bears out this observation. The U.S. Department of Labor Consumer Expenditure Survey revealed that consumption rates of the American middle class between 2000 through 2005 grew as quickly as the consumption rates of the highest income category. In fact, the increase in consumption rates for the American middle class was twice what it had been from 1990 to 1994. This transpired despite the loss of income for a typical household headed by a college graduate in this period. There was a similar increase in consumption in 2006.[10]

One factor that accounts for these higher consumption patterns relates to the American mania for shopping. The most recent survey of shopping-related travel by the U.S. Department of Transportation confirmed this. While in 1990 the typical car-owning family made 341 shopping trips, averaging 5.1 miles per trip, in 2001, this same American consumer made 496 shopping trips at an average length of 7 miles. Little has substantially changed about our shopping mania in this decade, even with the current recession and the inflation that these statistics preceded. No surprise about the results of these consumption and shopping patterns: America's middle class is drowning in debt, as its debt burden grew astronomically between 2001 and 2008. By the second quarter of 2008, household debt exceeded disposable income by 129.3 percent.[11] The Narcissistic lifestyle and its associated unfortunate outcomes have opened the American public to yearn for alternatives. It is this yearning that has led 85 percent of Americans polled as recently as 2004 in a survey by Widmeyer Communications to contend that society's values are out of whack and for more than half (53 percent) to express a willingness to forfeit one day's pay per week to have the day off to spend with family and friends. This assessment of our present moral climate was echoed in the results of a more recent 2008 Gallup poll.[12] These sentiments and the associated discontent with the Narcissist lifestyle comprise the need that Warren seeks to fill so skillfully with his formula for a life with purpose.

In fact, though, the typical American expressing such unhappiness with Narcissism has simply retreated into a cocoon of bigger, more ostentatious houses, all the while continuing to pursue pleasure-filled domesticity spiced with distracting entertainments and outsourcing family life whenever it is inconvenient or unfulfilling.[13] Clearly Narcissism helps account for the fragility of families today (as in 2002, half of first marriages were ending in divorce, a fivefold increase in the number of divorces since 1950) and Americans' permissive sexual attitudes (as 42 percent approve of extramarital sex [approved of by an even higher percentage of Generation Xers] and at least 50 percent say it is acceptable to cohabit).[14] The Narcissist pursuit of self-fulfillment has certainly not been quenched by the new domesticity.

Even the way we raise kids still reflects Narcissistic dispositions. In order to have our needs met or to make more money to maintain our consumption patterns, over 50 percent of all children were in some sort of non-parental care. Over 20 percent of children from fourth to eighth grade took care of themselves before and after school, and even 3 percent of kindergarteners through third graders were in that category.[15] Such an abdication of parental responsibility is further manifest in reports that in 2005 parents spent twenty-two less hours a week with their children than did parents in the 1960s, and that just a little less than one-third of America's children never eat a family meal with both parents. Having a television in each child's room (as is the case for 61 percent of American children) is an additional factor contributing to the trimming of parental time with children.[16] Overscheduling their children's involvement in numerous enrichment classes and youth sports further frees up parents' time.

The Narcissist immersion in America's therapeutic culture is even evident in these parenting styles. At least to some extent in order to assuage the guilt of not spending enough time with the kids, and also because our therapeutic ethos teaches us to encourage self-esteem, most American parents will praise their kids for everything, without mixing in much discipline. These days everybody receives an award at the inevitable banquet that concludes a season of organized children's activities. This sort of indulgence, psychologists like Ron Taffel note, nurtures children who are praise-addicts and so less motivated to do well at tasks leading to long-term lack of confidence. Those with high self-esteem are likely to be less inhibited and more willing to disregard risks.[17] Narcissistically inclined parents raise Narcissistic kids.

Rick Warren's vision of a purpose-driven life aims to minister in this context, to address our Narcissist tendencies. For all his good intentions, though, it is not clear he succeeds in proclaiming a version of the Gospel that overcomes and critiques such Narcissism.

A Purpose-Driven Theology

Rick Warren's God-centeredness clearly moves in a hopeful direction to critique and curtail contemporary American Narcissism. This orientation reflects in his call to readers, in the best traditions of American Puritanism, to live lives of praise and continuous thanks.[18] This sort of God-centeredness is certainly a promising remedy to the me-ism of our Narcissist ethos. Unfortunately the way in which Warren develops the theme of purpose is not as adequate to the task as we might wish.

Warren describes five purposes of human life: (1) Bringing enjoyment to God (through worshipping Him and becoming best friends with Him); (2) becoming an active part of God's family (through receiving Baptism and joining a church); (3) behaving like Christ by allowing ourselves to be molded by God's Word, by God's people, and by resisting temptations; (4) serving God (through using what God gave us to do good works, while becoming selfless and humble); and (5) acting as God's missionaries in the world (through engaging in evangelism activities).[19] His emphasis on purpose is a good counter to our society of self-promotion prevailing today. He does this well by stressing that we are to be servants, regarding no task as beneath us.[20]

Subsequent exposition of purpose may not be so fruitful for posing a countercultural alternative to the Narcissist winds that blow in contemporary American society. Though not problematic in itself, the eminent megachurch pastor turns to purpose in terms of what's in it for you—simplifying life, giving it meaning, focus, and motivation.[21] This observation could suggest an affirmation of the Narcissist preoccupation with self, a tendency to evaluate all things (even religious commitments) in terms of "what's in it for me." Could part of the reason for Rick Warren's success have to do with the possibility that, contrary to his intentions, but no less so than in the case of Prosperity Gospel proponents like Joel Osteen, he has presented a version of Christian faith palatable to Narcissist sensibilities, that we like him so much because he and his version of the faith meet our needs? This is a question that will pester us again and again throughout this book and ultimately accounts for my need to offer an alternative to Warren's purpose-driven vision.

Mandates to Purpose: What Has Become of Grace?

Another range of concerns I have with the purpose-driven model, a series of convictions that I will subsequently demonstrate in this chapter also account for Warren's impact on America, emerge from how he talks about living with purpose. Most of the time Rick Warren talks about purpose in terms of mandates (what we should do), not in terms of what God does to us and for us. Examples abound. Christians must obey God, Warren contends. He does make a very nice qualification in making this particular point: along with the best traditions of the Reformation, he contends that we are to obey God not out of duty or fear or compulsion, but because we love Him.[22] Unfortunately, Warren rarely reiterates this point, and as a result gives readers the impression that unless people do what he prescribes they are of no use to God.[23]

We see these trends in his discussion of evangelism. This ministry is said to be mandatory. And it is mandated that all members of his Saddleback Church must do some evangelism work as well as contribute regularly to the congregation. Elsewhere Warren contends that spiritual growth is not automatic. Growth in grace is said to be a decision we must make. You must decide to grow in grace, he asserts.[24] Again and again the language used to describe our purpose is the imperative form, speaking of what we must do. Reading God's Word is said to be useless if we do not put it into practice.[25]

Of course, Warren does assert that God has given each of us a shape. But he proceeds to add that it is up to us to develop that shape. And at many points he makes such a claim with no reference to the work or even assistance of the Holy Spirit.[26]

To his credit at least at one point the purpose-driven author clearly asserts that it is the Spirit's work to make us Christlike. Yet even in the exposition for that Day he refers to the need to cooperate with the Spirit. In his most recent book, *The Purpose of Christmas*, Warren even stresses justification by faith. Salvation is "done," he claims, not based on what we "do." But he proceeds to compromise these grace-filled assertions when he refers to the necessity of the believer's cooperation by our role in "trusting" or "relaxing." And in the same vein in the 2009 Martin Luther King, Jr. Annual Commemorative Service in Atlanta, he claimed that you need to be available for God to use you.[27] With the Protestant Reformers we must ask whether we can ever be sure we have cooperated, trusted, or been available enough?

Rick Warren practices what he preaches. His reliance on mandates to nurture Christian life (what is known in classical Protestant theology as the Third Use of the Law [the Commandments of God used for purposes of exhorting Christians to live the Christian life]) surfaces in covenants which every member of Saddleback Church signs. Among other commitments, members of his congregation promise to protect the unity of the church's fellowship. Also included in the covenant, as we have noted, is the pledge to make regular contributions to the church as well as to do mission work locally or abroad.[28]

Warren's propensity to issue mandates for encouraging the practice of the purpose-driven life leads him to go so far as to claim that "If you want God's blessing on your life and you want to be known as a child of God, you must learn to be a peacemaker."[29] He even claims that God rewards faithfulness in eternity. Those who did not help others will lose eternal rewards, it is claimed. Warren's belief in a God who judges also manifests in his assertion that the problems in life happen with God's permission or that God sends us frustrations in order to get us to change. More recently he has modified this a little, claiming that God's will is not always done, but then in turn referring to God allowing us freedom to go wrong, yet still contending that we are to turn to God as He is in ultimate control. This sort of rhetoric, witnessing to a contingent love of God, is evident in another Christian movement of great recent social impact, the Prosperity Gospel. The movement's most prominent spokesperson, Joel Osteen, claims that if we change our thinking or proceed with the right motives, God will open doors.[30]

True enough, Warren and Osteen are correct in contending that the Bible teaches these points. But the Reformation was about reminding the Church that these texts do not have the final Word, that the final Word is about God's grace and love (Galatians 3:10–13; Romans 3:21–26).[31] In fact, Rick Warren is flirting in these texts with a heresy of the early Church termed Pelagianism (the idea that we can merit salvation by how we live).

In a manner suggestive of the Pelagian heresy, Warren does not posit a strong doctrine of Sin. For example, he refers to our weaknesses without even mentioning sin and even contends that temptations are not sin. This weakening of the doctrine of Sin is also evident in his claim that our work does not have to be perfect for God to bless what we do. It is sufficient that it be just "good enough."[32] Reformation understandings of the Law of God clearly assert that God demands total, perfect obedience (Galatians 3:22).[33] The supposition is, as St. Paul contends, that all we are must be condemned as sin in order that all the promises of God would be given by grace through faith. To compromise the radical character of God's demands and our sinfulness is to compromise God's grace.

Such compromising of sin and so of the radicality of grace rears its ugly head at several other points. Thus Warren claims that often feelings of abandonment or estrangement from God, just like temptations, are said to have nothing to do with sin. They are just tests of faith.[34]

These same inclinations surface in the way in which this advocate of purpose-driven living talks about the significance of our missions. He claims that they have eternal significance.[35] This is true enough for any theologian rooted in the thought of the great Reformers and of their chief inspiration, the early African theologian St. Augustine. All of them agreed (in a manner most suggestive of Albert Einstein's Theory of Relativity) that there is a reality (in their case God is that reality) where there is no time, where all events are simultaneous, such that no event is ever lost.[36]

If this is what Warren intends by his claim about the eternal significance of the mission of the faithful he is to be commended. But he does not make clear that our earthly contributions to Christ's mission are at best ambiguous contributions, clouded by our sin. To this extent, Warren is too arrogant on this matter for me. Besides, his forgetting how our sin renders what we do to be of only ambiguously eternal significance, that what good comes out of what we do only becomes good because God makes use of it, entails that he and those following his vision are not totally dependent on God's grace.

Other examples of the guru of Purpose compromising grace should be cited. We see this in his advice for "defeating temptation," that we not allow it to trash into our minds, that we monitor media intake, and then "with the help of the Holy Spirit" reprogram the way we think.[37] It seems as if the Spirit will "help" if we do our part, another commitment shared by Prosperity Gospel preaching. It was precisely this sort of teaching by certain eminent theologians of the late Medieval Catholic Church (the school of Nominalism) against which the Reformers reacted in seeking their Reform.[38]

Elsewhere Warren speaks of the need to remove and replace our old habits, patterns, and practices. In this instance there is no reference to the Spirit's work. In a more recent book he calls on readers to "let God give you a new purpose," to cooperate, or to let Him work in us, but that God has left it up to us to accept our purpose.[39]

Rick Warren's and Prosperity Gospel preachers' preoccupation with exhorting Christian living is too often inclined to forget grace. As such, they wind up directing a lot of attention to us, and not to God, contrary to his intentions. Warren has not been brave enough in his commitments, both with regard to a ministry that will undermine our social Narcissism and also not brave enough in proclaiming our sin. Failure to do the latter entails leaving Narcissism alone. Because as long as there is something left in us that is good, the Narcissist inclination to take charge and make the world revolve around ourselves will continue to thrive, only this time in the name of Christian faith. The fact that Narcissist inclinations are not totally rejected by Warren and Prosperity Gospel preachers like Joel Osteen may contribute to their popularity, as they embody a "Christianity light"—a way of embracing faith without sacrificing too much and getting some fresh, affirming experiences, all the while being made to feel like you and what you do are important and have value. In the next chapter, I'll develop this theme further, as a way of making clearer why Warren's vision of the faith is not sufficient for changing American life, why we need the alternative I propose.

However, to attribute Rick Warren's popularity on the American scene merely to his failure fully to repudiate of our Narcissist ethos, to his ability to synthesize its preoccupation with the self with the Christian faith, is only part of the story. The main themes of Warren's purpose-driven vision are in line with the dominant emphases of the prevailing strands of American spirituality. We see this in his preoccupation with what we are to do to fulfill the divine mandates of our purpose (the good old-fashioned Protestant work ethic), the affirmation of free will implied by this conviction, a relegation of religion essentially to the private sphere of transforming individuals, and yet combining this with a sense that everything that transpires, even the bad things, are works of God. These convictions represent several of the main themes of a Puritanism modified by the Revivalism of the late nineteenth and twentieth centuries that has dictated the agenda of American religious sentiments. When we clarify the precise character of this dominant way of being religious in America, it will become more apparent how Warren's ability to tap into these themes are in large part what makes him such a force in our society as well as in cultures influenced by the American economy and its suppositions. Rick Warren's purpose-driven model of Christianity speaks the language of the American public, is the way religion should be done from an American perspective. Little wonder then he is having such an impact.

THE PURITAN-REVIVALIST CHARACTER OF AMERICAN SPIRITUALITY

Several prominent scholars of American religion have contended that it is not possible to understand religious phenomena on U.S. soil apart from a recognition that much of what has happened and still happens in America is driven by a Puritan Paradigm.[40] Essentially this entails that Puritanism has provided the primary categories for understanding American religiosity, that Americans tend to understand religion—even their own religious convictions—in terms of these categories.

Puritanism and Its Faith
Puritanism is a late-sixteenth/early-seventeenth-century Protestant movement originating in England, committed to purifying The

Church of England of all its Catholic vestiges. Although perse-
cuted in its earliest stages Puritans actually succeeded for a time,
even overthrowing the English King Charles I and briefly establishing a republic.

A movement clearly indebted theologically to the sixteenth-
century Reformer of Geneva John Calvin, Puritanism affirmed the
sovereignty of God and portrayed him as an electing God in total
control.[41] This set of beliefs continues to appear in contemporary
America; as for all our belief in American freedom, whenever natural cataclysms transpire people will be heard to say that they have
been sent by God. Warren may not teach predestination, but we
have noted his belief that God sends temptations to us. Likewise,
predestination continues to hover around the American spiritual
psyche as we tend to think of ourselves and our nation as chosen
people living in a promised land with a mission of bringing freedom to the world. At least this was the essence of George Bush's
foreign policy. Warren's idea of having a mission of eternal significance links with this idea of the faithful's exceptionalism.

In order to ensure confidence that the faithful are truly God's
elect, Puritans taught that good works that ensue from obedience
to God's Law "are fruits and evidences of a true and lively faith."[42]
To be a Puritan is to live a life of assiduous obedience to what God
has ordained, knowing that the work one does is a sign of faith and
election. This sort of lifestyle seems to nurture the ideal laborer for a
growing capitalist economy. No accident. The earliest supporters of
the Puritan moment in England were proponents of the capitalist revolution, with not much use for government programs to support the
poor.[43] Puritanism has been good for American business and makes
religious Americans suspicious of big government safety nets.[44]

Along with our heritage of freedom the Puritan legacy leads
most Americans to think of religion in terms of good moral behavior in accord with the teachings of the Ten Commandments.
This emphasis reflects in America today, as a poll conducted as
recently as 2001 by the Barna Research Group revealed that seven

in ten Americans believe that good works contribute to our salvation.[45] Rick Warren's vision of a purpose-driven life along with Joel Osteen's Prosperity Gospel, with their focus on mandates for Christian living and even their Pelagian tendencies, clearly harmonize with this set of commitments. They embody these Puritan/American convictions. Little wonder these visions should resonate so well in American society.

Other Puritan beliefs included a theologically conservative view of the Bible, a belief that faith commitments should impact society, along with views of worship and the Sacraments that broke with Roman Catholic beliefs. The Puritan way of worship, stressing reverence and solemnity without much emphasis on the Sacraments, has been clearly reflected in American attitudes. Thus according to a 2006 poll of the Pew Forum on Religion & Public Life, 35 percent of Americans still believe the Bible to be the literal Word of God (76 percent of Americans claim it to be God's Word in some sense) and one-third of the public (two-thirds of the public who worship weekly) would rather have the Bible influence the laws than the Constitution. Even the election dynamics of 2008 did not erode the commitment to the role of religion in politics too drastically (a loss of about twenty percentage points).[46] As for styles of worship, for most Americans of European ethnic background (and among minorities who have assimilated), to be religious means to be serious and disciplined, not unduly joyful. When Christian worship is portrayed in the media, such as in the ultra-successful TV comedy, *The Simpsons*, it is a nonliturgical (Puritanlike) rite that the viewers see.

One additional conviction of the Puritans, which has had a major impact on American history though less so on the American social psyche since World War II, has been their affirmation of the thoroughgoing sinfulness of fallen human nature.[47] This concept clearly reflects in our Constitutional system and its separation of powers. Though not very well recognized by many commentators, something like the concept of Original Sin derived from Puritan

antecedents underlies much of the literature of the founders in
support of the idea of the three branches of government. James
Madison, Secretary of the Constitutional convention, was greatly
influenced by his teacher at the College of New Jersey (today
Princeton University) John Witherspoon, the only clergyman to
sign The Declaration of Independence and himself a committed Puritan/Presbyterian who during Madison's student days had
advocated a separation of powers in three branches because of
Original Sin.[48] As we have already observed, today this commitment is not as essential to the way Americans view themselves, as
now so many believe they are good enough to qualify for heaven
on their own. As recently as 2000, 73 percent of Americans
believed we are born good.[49]

We will note shortly that this departure from Puritan convictions is in part a function of the way in which the Puritan Paradigm
was modified by the impact of Revivalism on the American social
psyche. Such a positive self-image also relates more readily with the
impact of the therapeutic ethos on American society today. It also
helps explain why so many Americans are Constitutionally ignorant
and not very interested in politics. Politics reveals the seedy side of
human nature. This may explain both why Rick Warren and his
Prosperity Gospel colleagues in ministry compromise the doctrine
of Sin in favor of what we are to do and also have not used their
pulpits to pressure politicians. Subsequently, we'll explore this point
further. First, though, let's examine in some detail how Puritan suppositions have impacted American life and thinking about religion.

Impact of Puritanism on America

It is no accident that in the popular mind American history (except
for Columbus's "discovery" of America) begins with the 1620 land-
ing of the Pilgrims, who were of the Puritan persuasion. After the
same fashion, one of the major American holidays, Thanksgiving,
is at least mythologically rooted in Puritan piety.

In all sorts of ways, Puritanism has and continues to have an

impact on American life. Some of the oldest and still most presti-
gious American churches are those First Congregational churches
(affiliated with the United Church of Christ today) in the various
cites and towns of New England which have roots in the Puritan
heritage. Membership in these congregations does nothing to hurt
your social standing and business contacts. Likewise, in the South
it never hurts to belong to the town's First Baptist Church. Baptists,
recall, have their origins in the Puritan movement and continue to
embody most of the original Puritan convictions.[50] Even if you did
not grow up in such congregations, it is decidedly to your advantage economically, socially, and politically to belong to them.

Other Puritan-rooted denominations that are acknowledged as
truly American include Presbyterianism and in a derived sense The
Episcopal Church and The United Methodist Church. Puritanism,
recall, originated in The Church of England (the mother church
of American Episcopalianism). With regard to Methodism, we
must remember that the parents of John Wesley, the movement's
founder, were raised in the Puritan ethos, so that much Reformed
thinking is embedded in the Wesleyan heritage.

In view of these dynamics it is hardly surprising that most
American elites belong to these "truly American" churches of the
Puritan Paradigm. Most American presidents have belonged to
these denominations, including the last six. In the 110th Congress,
222 seats were held by members of one of the denominations associated with The Puritan Paradigm. By contrast, denominations
or religious persuasions not associated with the Puritan Paradigm
(like Jews, Muslims, Catholics, Lutherans, Pentecostals, Eastern
Orthodox Christians, African Methodist Episcopal) have collectively only had one president (the Catholic John Kennedy). Among
this group the 110th Congress only included 43 Jews, 17 Lutheran
members (the third largest denomination in the country), and
only 70 Catholics (the largest denomination in the nation). It is
evident that real power and influence rests with the denominations embodying Puritan convictions. That is because its beliefs and

practices effectively define the American (religious) way.

Given these social pressures, it is not surprising that the Puritan ethos has had an impact on the adherents of the religious bodies just noted. Perhaps even against their wills, these religiously oriented Americans may begin to conform their communities ever so gradually to the prevailing attitudes until even people in churches with non-Puritan traditions begin to work and act like Puritans. Examples include the way in which segments of the American Jewish community have put more emphasis on Hanukkah than has been typical in the Jewish tradition as a result of the importance that another December festival (Christmas) holds for parishioners of Puritan Paradigm churches and other Americans.

We can also observe these dynamics in operation in the diminution of liturgical worship and the infrequency of celebrations of the Sacrament of the Lord's Supper in certain non-Puritan traditions. American Lutheranism provides a good example. Like Jews, most ethnic Lutherans in America wanted to become "American" (as defined by Puritanism), and so a significant number of its congregations gave up use of the historic liturgy and celebrated the Sacrament of the Lord's Supper infrequently. Many Lutherans have also forfeited the historic understanding of the Sacrament as well as adopted a vision of Christian responsibility more like the Puritans and Rick Warren's than Martin Luther's. Even in some African-American churches, traditionally typified by a celebrative worship style, one experiences something more characteristic of Puritan sobriety. The pressures on these religious groups are to conform to Puritan ways, because most Americans operate that way and especially the majority of these elites who remain religious or who depict religion in the media. It is in this sense that we can refer to a Puritan Paradigm for American religion. A religious leader (as well as political leaders like George Bush and other Neo-Conservatives) who can tap into these themes, as Rick Warren and Joel Osteen have, will connect with broad segments of the American public.

Of course, we need to clarify that the Puritan Paradigm of American religion is not identical with what the original Puritans taught and practiced. We have already noted that the original Puritans had a strong social vision and hoped to establish a society that would advance the Christian religion (a commitment stated in the Mayflower Compact). There was no sense of religion only being a matter of the private sphere as many Americans have today. Perhaps the First Amendment contributes to this rethinking of the Puritan Paradigm. But the most significant factor in altering America's Puritan Paradigm from the original version of Puritanism has been the impact of late-nineteenth and early-twentieth-century Revivalism on the American social psyche. It has effectively privatized the view of religion of most Americans.

American Revivalism and Its Impact on the Puritan Paradigm
Post–Civil War America was in crisis, while at the same time beginning to transform itself into the global superpower it would become in the next century. American industry was starting to boom in the North. Immigrants and transplants from rural areas were streaming into northern cities to man the factories. Among longtime residents the new economic circumstances and changing population patterns made many feel that they were losing their way of life, if not their nation. Declining morality was also evidenced, especially among the new "urban immigrants." Coming from impoverished or rural areas, the temptations of the big city were clearly affecting these urban immigrants' daily lives. Church life suffered under these circumstances. Although the rate of moral decay was still a long way from the secularism we have experienced in the second half of the twentieth and in the present centuries, there was much lamenting about the nation turning from Jesus. The young were not receiving the sort of Christian training they had in previous generations.

Post-bellum America yearned for a revival. Of course there had already been two great revivals on American soil—the Great

Awakening of the Colonial Era and the Second Great Awakening of the pre–Civil War decades of the nineteenth century. Prayers were answered in the revivals of Dwight Lyman Moody (1837–1899) and later by Billy Sunday (1862–1935), whose primary heir has been Billy Graham. Collectively they have had significant impact on the American religious and social psyche.

All three of these great Revivalists and those they have influenced embodied many of the suppositions of the Puritan Paradigm. In part, that is why they impacted American life as much as they did. All three place much emphasis on the individual Christian's responsibility. Where they differed from the original Puritans was that they have placed so much emphasis on that theme as to compromise a belief in the sovereignty of God and predestination in favor of embracing belief in human free will.[51] In an intriguing way this dimension of their thought both has and has not transformed the Puritan Paradigm. We have already noted how Americans love free will, but in emergencies, if not most of the time, it seems that 69 percent of us are like the early Puritans—ready to attribute all events to the Will of God. We have observed that most of the time Rick Warren aligns himself with this line of thought.[52]

The Revivalist teaching of free will entails that we can do something to make ourselves good, for we can will to be born again. This is of course a compromise of the Puritan conception of human nature as corrupt and sinful. We have already called attention to how this Revivalist conviction has had a significant impact on the American social psyche, with so many Americans today feeling good about themselves and their "basic decency." It has found such a resonance among Americans in part because it connected with the Founders' stress on freedom and the endorsement of deism by some of them (the so-called Jeffersonian, "Secular-Democratic" strand of the American political system).[53] We have also previously noted Rick Warren's and Prosperity Gospel preacher Joel Osteen's propensity to endorse this sort of optimistic assessment of human nature. Neo-Conservatism and the Religious Right have also endorsed this theme, and even some conservative/centrist Democrats find it amenable. The ability to tap into this particular Revivalist amendment of the Puritan Paradigm has contributed to the success of each of them. Since people are thought to be fundamentally good, and the public believes it, government regulations and Christian prophecy pertaining to the social and political structures are not deemed necessary. Advocacy of small government is the likely result of optimism about human nature.

Another emphasis not as clearly evident in historic Puritanism was the Revivalist stress on being born again and coming to Christ.[54] This distancing from historic Puritanism in turn has manifested in a vision of the Revivalism as a ministry directed to the transformation of individuals (to saving souls), not to transforming society as a whole as the earlier revival leaders of the Awakenings intended.[55] Of course, these commitments are hardly surprising given the fact that Moody and Sunday in particular had close ties to the business establishment. As a result, a vision of Christianity they and Graham have espoused that did not intervene in the political realm entailed that Christian faith would not get in the way of the market. Just what the business community wanted.

Given the impact of these Revivalists and their institutions, this vision of Christian faith would in time prevail on large segments of American society, transforming the Puritan Paradigm and the way in which most Americans think about religion. We have already suggested how these dynamics account for the success the Right had politically in recent years by aligning itself with the core commitments of this amended version of the Puritan Paradigm.[56] I will now note in more detail how this also helps account for Rick Warren's as well as Prosperity Gospel's impact. Warren too has skillfully tapped into the main strands of the Revivalist-amended Puritan Paradigm.

SUMMARY:
RICK WARREN AND
THE PURITAN PARADIGM

It is now evident that Rick Warren, trained and raised in the Puritan-inspired Baptist tradition, embodies most of the central commitments of the Revivalist-amended Puritan Paradigm. Most of these points of contact we have previously noted. We have highlighted his Puritanlike preoccupation with our responsibility to fulfill the divine mandates of our purpose, affirmation of free will, and his paradoxical affirmation of a God in control of everything that transpires. Our consideration of the way in which Revivalism has transformed the American spiritual psyche also reveals two other ways in which Warren has aligned himself with core commitments of the Puritan Paradigm. Revivalists, noted earlier, stress the born-again experience. True to his Baptist roots, Warren refers to Baptism, not in the Sacramental sense of Catholics or even Lutherans, but as a symbol of a prior commitment.[57] In linking with the born-again emphasis of the Revivalists we observe again how Warren links himself with characteristically American themes.

One more way in which Warren links with the Revivalist-transformed Puritan Paradigm pertains to the Revivalist focus on transforming individuals, not society. For all his concern with overcoming the individualism of our social Narcissism, Rick Warren largely shares the Revivalist privatizing of religion. To be sure, privatizing is not Warren's intention. His crusade against Narcissism leads him to lament that a lack of community, a sense of whether anyone counts on "me," has been lost. Of course, he addresses this nicely to some extent with his insistence on the essential character of the Church for the purpose-driven life.[58] But in line with the politics that have preoccupied America since the Reagan Revolution, this community that Warren posits (the Church) is more a refuge from the world, not a community committed structurally to changing the world and remedying its exploitative practices. Could we say he has reduced the Church to a community that meets my needs, or at least one that meets the needs of my fellow members or friends?

In fact this renown megachurch pastor seems to answer the preceding question affirmatively as he almost explicitly divorces involvement in this community from the world with the way in which he interprets 1 Peter 2:17 and Galatians 6:10. He uses these texts to authorize his conclusion that the Church and its members to which Christians belong is to receive special attention and extra love in comparison to love given to the rest of the world.[59] In fact, Warren cannot make his point with regard to the Petrine text's original Greek, and the second text only refers to members of the Church as a venue for exercising love for all.

Warren's concentration on your and my purpose seems further to contribute to the privatizing of religion. This is evident in the fact that in his biggest seller, even when referring to the mission of Christians, he does not refer to political engagement on behalf of the poor or for the sake of peace.[60] It is to his credit that since writing *The Purpose Driven Life* Warren has engaged himself and his ministry in a most promising outreach to fighting AIDS in Africa and his global P.E.A.C.E. Plan,[61] which will endeavor to marshal resources of his own megachurch and the millions of American Christians he influences to try to turn every Christian congregation worldwide into a provider of health care, literacy, and economic development. But even in these ministries he has not been inclined, except in one 2005 open letter, to pressure the political sphere to facilitate these changes, and has not used his significant influence or recruited his important network of supporters to push Congress and the Administration or foreign governments to commit to helping the AIDS crisis or to overcoming poverty. He doesn't do politics, he claims.[62]

An even stronger affirmation of a laissez-faire view of government and economics is espoused by Joel Osteen and his Prosperity

Gospel allies, as they unequivocally affirm free-market dynamics. The shared Revivalist commitment to focusing faith on personal transformation and to keeping religion out of politics is even evident in Warren's and Osteen's hesitancy about enunciating or advocating their common critical perspective on homosexuality. Warren's support of California's ban of gay marriage passed in the 2008 elections was announced only ten days prior to the election and only on a website targeting members of his church.[63] The Revivalist transformation of America's Puritan Paradigm and its conservative sociopolitical implications are clearly alive and well in the thought and ministries of Rick Warren as well as of the Prosperity Gospel preachers.

The last observation makes it evident again how Rick Warren's views are in line with the American way of life. He truly is America's preacher in that sense; perhaps we could deem him the next Billy Graham. Little wonder he is so popular in view of how much he embodies American values and its vision of the way religion should be done. That is just the problem, I contend. Like proponents of the Prosperity Gospel, Rick Warren is so in line with the American way of life that his purpose-driven model of life is too American, not equipped to transform American society or even to address the Narcissism and self-centeredness that plagues America and Western society today. We'll elaborate further on this point in the next chapter.

How Purpose-Driven
Living Can Lead to a Life
That's All about You
The Burden of Self-Centeredness

Along with proponents of the Prosperity Gospel, Rick Warren truly embodies an American piety. This may account for his present popularity and impact. But sometimes when you share too much in common with the establishment you forfeit your ability to be prophetic. In this chapter we'll see that, despite his good intentions, this is the case with Warren. As much as Joel Osteen and other Prosperity Gospel proponents, we will see how Warren's focus on our purpose readily leads to the risk of relegating faith to an experience that is primarily about what we can get out of it for ourselves. In so doing, he and the Prosperity Gospel preachers nurture a lifestyle that is readily co-opted by the dominant Narcissist ethos of the contemporary American context.

Warren's failures on this score are not peculiar to his own purpose-driven theological perspective. They are symptomatic of the general failure of the main streams of American Christianity, influenced by the Revivalist-inspired Puritan Paradigm, to respond to the Narcissism of our times and to the economic dynamics which have nurtured it. But first we need to clarify the incestuous relationship between our Narcissist ethos and the business dynamics of contemporary American society.

NARCISSISM, OUR ECONOMIC ETHOS, AND THE PURITAN PARADIGM: THE MONOPLY THIS PARTNERSHIP HAS ON AMERICAN LIFE

The globalized economy of the twenty-first century clearly lends itself to connecting with the Narcissist personality of post-1950s America. In an economy like ours is today (what Thomas Friedman has called the "flat world"), characterized by flexibility, openness to new ideas, and strong interpersonal networking skills, there is little use for community and traditions bigger than the self.[1] Reinvention, experiencing what is novel, is the name of the game. These dynamics do not just explain the lack of corporate loyalty to employees, the American labor force's propensity to change jobs regularly, but they also relate to our maniacal consumption patterns mentioned in the first chapter.[2] In a society where the norm is to find self-fulfillment at all costs, to make everything and everyone a vehicle for meeting the individual's needs, people need something to fill the void they sense. Obtaining the latest niche-marketed, customized goods, the big car (the SUV), or the big house (neither of which you can really afford) is a way of filling the void (or at least of trying to fill the void, because the latest fashion will soon make what I have less valuable, especially for Narcissists who live only for present gratification). Another way Americans caught up in these dynamics seek to fill their emptiness is with celebrities (of the media or the athletic field), and so we seek to emulate them in lifestyle and with the things we acquire.[3]

Computer technology and the new ethos of the corporation further nurture a Narcissist social climate. Intelligence in using machines is dull when the interest is operation rather than self-critical, as has been typical of American industry since the dawn of the assembly line. When I am skilled only in making the machine work, when I am not interested in how the machine affects society and how it might be used differently, or when I am not even willing to challenge its use, my expertise is merely routine and therefore dulled by routine. I do not need to think; I am no longer challenged. I know *how* to do things, not *why* I do them. Computers have intensified these dynamics. They provide answers, but not necessarily understanding of the answer provided. I have the answer from the computer without knowing why it is the right answer. The dynamics entail that I am detached or removed from the work undertaken on the computer. It is not quite mine. I passively receive data or have the mathematical equation figured out for me. I do not have to do much research myself, save my mastery of the machine. With regard to the actual subject of the problem considered, I am a mere spectator, not the problem solver.[4]

Such passivity is not good for society. Because I am only loosely connected to the job I do, it does not define me. I really do not know who I am. A sense of identity and historical continuity with the self is lost by such business dynamics, nurturing a trait most symptomatic of the Narcissist.[5] Of course in another sense this loss of identity is good for business. It nurtures a sense of emptiness in the buying public and makes them better targets for advertising the latest must-see movie or must-have product.

The nurturing of such emptiness and lack of self-continuity is exacerbated by American business' commitment to flexibility that renders job security a reality of a bygone era, and also by the style of management which prevails in most Fortune 500 companies. The cornerstone of modern management practice is the belief that loose networks are more open to decisive reinvention than are pyramidal hierarchies.[6] Teams are created for short-term tasks. Long-term in business is not good for flexibility, a commitment so crucial to the new economy.

The modern team is flexible, able to deal with new circumstances and then move on the next issue. In keeping with the egalitarian ethos of post-1960 America and our therapeutic ethos, the team does not acknowledge differences in privileges or power. In our therapeutic ethos, inclined as most Americans are to interpret their lives at least subliminally in the categories of psychology, conflict is a bad thing. But in fact just the opposite of egalitarianism and shared power results. I cannot trust my teammates in today's flexible economy. They are out to get the promotion I want, even to have my job. In such a climate I am not likely to make real, lifelong friends on the job. I will remain isolated. My voice will also be silenced by those in power on teams created in this ethos. In a culture where disagreement and conflict are discouraged, the boss can silence dissent, even co-opting fellow workers to his side, ostensibly in the interest of team harmony but in reality in the interest of advancing the boss's own manipulative power.

As a result the good team player is flexible, not fully invested in any particular values or decisions of the team or even of the organization. He or she is ironic about life. Such team players (employees and managers) must be good listeners, willing to share without appearing to exercise power. In short they must be good actors, manipulating others into wrongly believing that they are not pulling strings or using them to advance their careers. "Be nice in order to get what you want. But if someone's been nice to you, watch your butt."[7] When life is all about selling your personality as if it were a personality, you do not own yourself any longer, nor do you really determine how you are since all you do and say is geared to the reactions you are getting from supervisors and admirers. The paradox of the Narcissist is obviously in play once again. The new company man or woman is highly concentrated on himself or herself. But because I have no ownership of my actions or thoughts in such a business ethos, since what I say or do is a function of what the audience wants, the self is emptied in such an environment. And emptied as I am by such a life of performances for others (for the sake of my career), I'm likely to try to fill the emptiness with propaganda about how good or powerful I am, buy the latest must-have item, or take up some exciting affair (even if I am married). To heck with others; they are just vehicles for my pleasure. Contemporary business practice furthers American Narcissism.

Of course these dynamics are not totally new to the era of the computer revolution. The psychologization of the society and niche marketing had already begun in earnest after World War II. The universities and public education systems began to be saturated with German Enlightenment skepticism about absolute truth, and the Social Sciences (including and notably Psychology) began to permeate the curricular assumptions of these institutions.[8] American businesses began targeting the Baby Boom generation while it was still in diapers and the previous generation was still too young to fight in the war. Aided by the evolution of Rock & Roll, these businesses first created a whole youth culture distinct from that of the elders. Before the Computer Revolution, business had begun to change its older top-down managing systems and sense of responsibility for its workers (to provide them with lifetime jobs and a decent standard of living) to today's less worker-friendly, more flexible, and team-management style of administration.

Complicity of the Puritan Paradigm
In all these developments, especially beginning in the 1950s, business and American society as a whole had a significant ally in the dominant religion paradigm in the nation. I have already dealt with the origins of Puritanism. What needs to be highlighted again is that the movement began with pro–free market sympathizers and the first proponents held such a vision. This is authenticated by one of the movement's first generation of leaders, Richard Baxter (1615–1691). The last monarch in England prior to the Puritan Revolution's triumph had sought to create a safety net for the labor force and the poor. In response, Puritan leaders of the era like Richard Steele bashed the poor, contending that their poverty

was the result of their own idleness. These Puritan attitudes were transplanted to America. Premiere early American Puritan author and co-founder of Yale University Cotton Mather (1663–1728) observed that as Puritans proceeded in serving God they prospered materially.[9] Puritan religious convictions dispose you to free-market dispositions along with an intolerance toward those who don't make it in society.

This capitalist friendliness was also apparent in the first modern Revivalists, whose movement was so influential in modifying early America's Puritan dispositions. The great nineteenth-century Revivalist Dwight Moody, who influenced Billy Sunday and Billy Graham, was critical of the poor, and seemed to promise prosperity to those who follow Christ. Billy Sunday largely echoed these claims, contending once that "I never saw a Christian that was a hobo."[10] Even Billy Graham has been a proponent of small-government free-market strategies, as he has asserted that love and the spirit of Jesus are what we need to overcome poverty.[11] A Puritanism modified by Revivalist themes could not but nurture a lot of positive free-market sentiments among all those American faithful belonging to churches that shared these theological convictions.

To be sure, Puritanism's pro-capitalist propensities did not lead to individualism in the first century of the American Republic. The strong sense of community and the need for discipline that Puritanism emphasized kept wanton individualism in check. But modern Revivalism was itself geared to the individual, without much corporate concern.[12] When it merged with the capitalist suppositions of Puritanism in the American social psyche, American religion came to be an ally of the individualizing dynamics of business, especially when both mainline American religion and business began to endorse therapeutic modes of dealing with the world. Religiously inclined Americans would for the most part— with the exception of those religious groups not sharing the theological convictions of the Puritan Paradigm, like the historic Black church, Catholics, Lutherans, and Jews—become proponents of the free market and not challenge its development.[13] Such a theological perspective is also impotent to challenge the development of the Narcissist therapeutic dynamics I've described, especially since they seemed so closely liked to the business dynamics of the market. The partnership of the Puritan Paradigm and our economic ethos has effectively become a cultural monopoly, even among secularists. And when you share such a pro-business, individualistic perspective on reality, not much is going to get done to challenge structures that undergird our social Narcissism and the poverty or injustice associated with our economic system.

The Revivalist amending of the Puritan Paradigm further aggravated American religion's general uncritical approval of the technological and economic status quo to the extent that the revised Puritan Paradigm does not unequivocally endorse a sovereign God like the first Puritans did. In its place Revivalism tends to posit free will and a God (largely influenced by seventeenth-century Reformed theologian Jakob Arminius) who allows for human contributions, much like the God of America's Founders. These moves have allowed most Americans to continue to share the Puritan belief in American exceptionalism (that we are part of an elect nation) and the promise of a good life for those living Puritan capitalist values, but now no longer necessarily seen as established by God or biblical principles, since in freedom we may need to push them aside. Rather, for secular America our blessings are now more likely deemed to have been established by science or progress.[14] For secularism these are the new gods, the givers of our blessings.

How is the Church to respond to our contemporary ethos? When it comes to doing effective ministry in such a context, "If you can't lick 'em, join 'em," has become the effective watchword among religious leaders. As we've already established, the success of Rick Warren and his Prosperity Gospel counterpart Joel Osteen is largely a function of their sharing the characteristic theological themes of America's Revivalist-amended Puritan Paradigm. Linked

as they are to the Puritan Paradigm it is hardly surprising that
the characteristic themes of Warren and Osteen would not offer
much effective critique of our Narcissism and its alliance with the
American economy.

WHY PURPOSE-DRIVEN AND PROSPERITY MODELS CAN'T SET US FREE FROM OURSELVES

The construction of an alliance by proponents of the Prosperity
Gospel with the American business establishment is obvious.
Preachers like Joel Osteen emphasize in their ministries what
God can give, rather than God in himself. Life and even faith
are all about what's good for the individual, what's good for me.
Insalubrious trends in society are never criticized, save a warning
not to get too hung up on Narcissist "me-ims."[15] The fundamental
belief that prosperity (including the market's version of economic
prosperity) is a good is unquestioned. Locked as it is into the contemporary business ethos which fosters Narcissism, the Prosperity
Gospel seems to yoke the faithful to these same dynamics and
their Narcissistic outcomes.

At first glance, this critique seems not to apply to Rick Warren.
His concept of purpose starts with God and is closely linked to the
worship of God. But he proceeds to speak of the individual's own
purpose (*my purpose*) and even claims a little like the Prosperity
Gospel preachers that wonderful results follow when you get
God's plan in your heart and that God has created us *for success*.[16]
Contrary to his intentions it seems that Rick Warren has also not
liberated himself from the bondage of the self—interpreting all
reality (including God) in light of the self's own agenda. To reiterate a point noted in the previous chapter, it is noteworthy that
Warren's own writings tend to privatize religion. In his biggest
seller, even when referring to the mission of Christians, he does

not refer to political engagement on behalf of poverty or peace and does not refer to seeking change of unjust or exploitative economic institutions.[17] Nothing in the writings of Rick Warren, save a critique of defining oneself by what we own (he still contends that wealth can bring some happiness), indicates that he provides a theological perspective that allows us to critique the economic and social institutions that are encouraging our Narcissist self-centeredness.[18] Could his popularity and impact have something to do with the fact that he is not bearing really bad news, that his is a "light" critique of self-centeredness, one with which self-righteous Narcissists and ego-addicts can live?

To his credit, Osteen does contend that the focus of a life of prosperity ought not just to be on ourselves, but that we should become givers. Yet he still places a focus on the self, essentially claiming that you have to "do to get." How we treat others, he claims, can have a "great impact" on the degree of blessings and favor of God.[19] Osteen's God, like Warren's, it seems, has been subordinated to our own agendas. This is the essence of Narcissism, seeing everything and everyone as a vehicle for one's own self-gratification.

Perhaps we might try to offer a rebuttal of this critique, by pointing out again how Warren in particular, but even Osteen, tries to assert that the agendas of our purpose or prosperity are God-given. Such a transcendent perspective, it might be argued, embodies a critique of our social Narcissism.

Even if we grant this argument, given the fact that there is ambiguity about this matter, a careful reader might come away with the conclusion that both Warren and the Prosperity Gospel flirt with the reduction of God's agenda to our own. This ambiguity is problematic regarding the viability of these theological perspectives to afford us with a countercultural version of the faith in our own context. Given their lack of clarity at this point (concerning their ability to make clear that God's ways, the ways of Purpose and Prosperity, are not the world's ways), adherents of the theologies of Rick Warren as much as Joel Osteen are clearly susceptible to being co-opted by the Narcissist "me-first" agenda. Embedded in the presuppositions of the business-friendly Puritan Paradigm, their viewpoints do not provide them with a prophetic perspective with which to critique the socioeconomic dynamics we have been considering.

This line of criticism pertains not just to Warren and Osteen, but also to much of the theology that has dominated the American and European educational establishment since World War II, if not before. I contend that one of the reasons why the mainline Protestant and even Catholic churches have become less and less of a social force since the 1950s is that the dominant theological options of these denominations have been co-opted by suppositions that reduce Christian faith to a mere expression of the tastes of their adherents. This charge was made as early as 2000 by no less an eminent forum of analysis than the *Wall Street Journal.*[20]

Essentially what has transpired is that these denominations have embraced a style of theology largely indebted to the father of modern Christian theology, a German Evangelical named Friedrich Schleiermacher (1768–1834). Essentially Schleiermacher broke with the prevailing Protestant Orthodox models of theology of his day, which initiated theological reflection from the perspective of an inerrant Bible, and instead undertook an apology for Christianity by trying to relate it to the credible worldview of his day (i.e., Romantic philosophy).[21] This idea, that all that we do about God and the faith is relative to our contemporary experience, has become the way to do theology in these circles. Among the leaders of Protestant theology in the last century to embrace this approach include Paul Tillich, Rudolf Bultmann, and Paul Ricoeur, as well as two of the most prominent Catholic theologians of the postwar era. More recently this commitment has been made especially clear in various so-called Liberation Theologies, as God is deemed Black by James Cone and many Feminist Theologians portray God as female.[22]

These theological models are not well suited to critique the Narcissism of our day. They portray the elements of Christian faith, even God, in terms of our own agendas. Sure, that's what Americans seem to want, but not those whose lives have been shaped by the Bible's stories and concepts. In trying to make faith relevant they effectively trivialize it, since the American public as a whole can have all the self-seeking it wants without needing those religious trappings. Little wonder denominations endorsing this style of theology have been losing ground, while ecclesiastical communities associated with the Evangelical Movement rejecting these convictions have grown.[23] What is fascinating, though, is that while not sharing the hermeneutic (suppositions about how to interpret Scripture) of these more liberal mainstream academic theologians, Warren and Osteen are effectively doing the same thing with regard to submitting faith to our own agendas. Tune in again in twenty years to learn whether this strategy will lead to the popular negative perception that faith has been trivialized by prosperity and purpose-driven theologies as the mainline denominations now endure. In any case, this is not a theological approach that can readily liberate us from ourselves, or lift the burdens of self-centeredness. But there is another, more serious reason why these theologies fail. It has to do with their compromise of grace.

When Christian Life Becomes a Burden

Both Warren and Osteen share common problems in this regard. As I have observed, both minimize the role of grace in providing the good life (they are almost Pelagian in stressing our works) and correspondingly have a weak conception of sin.[24] I have mentioned that both agree that you have to do something in order to be blessed. Warren only speaks of faults, weaknesses, or mistakes, and Osteen only refers to barriers of the past, mistakes, or "disappointments." Neither of them actually refers to Romans 7:14–24 and original sin.

Such a diminution of sin is what the American public wants. As I mentioned in the previous chapter, statistics from a 2001 poll indicate that seven in ten Americans believe that good works contribute to our salvation. An earlier 2000 *New York Times* poll found that 73 percent of respondents believed people are born good and that 85 percent thought they could be pretty much whatever they wanted to be.[25]

Conformity to such cultural attitudes is in part a function of the Narcissism of our society, the desire for affirmation and to justify focus on the self. But such optimism about human nature is also rooted in the so-called Jeffersonian or Secular-Democratic (though not the Madisonian) strand of American society. (Recall that Jefferson and his Deist colleagues stressed individual freedom, virtue, and progress, while Madison's more pessimistic, Augustinian view of human nature prevailed in the Constitution's separation of powers.[26])

My contention is that these cultural attitudes help account for the success of both Warren and Osteen. Not saying much about sin and stressing our responsibility (not giving God's loving grace all the credit for the good in life) is what Americans caught up in our Narcissist ethos want to hear. Preachers today can tell stories of warnings they get from parishioners about preaching too much sin. It is not what today's Americans (or most denizens of Western society) want to hear. Of course human beings never did want to hear that message.

In particular, American Narcissists do not want to be reminded of their sin; that Word would call into question the validity of their self-seeking. Insecure and empty as they are, craving admiration, the last thing they want is to have the validity of their projects challenged, especially not in Church.

A theology downplaying sin will likely be popular in such a setting. But it won't be God-centered, stressing grace. What the purpose-driven theology of Warren does, and more so Osteen's Prosperity Gospel model, is present a theology that not only does not challenge our business climate, but also reinforces our Narcissism and self-centeredness. In an odd way, as legalistic as these theological proposals are (with all Warren's calls to obedience of God as well as other mandates and Osteen's demands that we have the right motives, even to receive divine blessings), they fail to teach the Law in its Theological Use.[27] They do not teach Galatians 3:10–14 and Paul's idea that to live according to the Law of God is a curse. Oddly enough in this neglect of the judgment of God, they unwittingly nurture more guilt.[28] For if my mandate is to change my mind-set in order to prosper and to have faith in order to activate the power of God (Osteen) or to accept the mandates of one's purpose (Warren), if I find that I am not materially blessed or find life meaningless, it must be my fault. I can't fall back on grace in these circumstances on the grounds of these theologies, because I have not done my part. This lack of unconditional affirmation by God is especially clear in Osteen, as contrary to his interventions to affirm the goodness of God, he advocates a portrayal of our Lord as judge of bad things that happen, as one whose blessings are contingent.[29] This is hardly surprising as viewed from the brave-sinning perspective I advocate. Martin Luther contended that without the condemning voice of God's Law one will not encounter the God of love.[30]

The respective emphases of Warren and Osteen on what we can get out of faith forfeit the transcendent perspective and full reliance on God's unconditional grace that we need in order to break with the misery and meaninglessness of a life centered on ourselves and in bondage to the socioeconomic trends I have been describing. Their theological proposals are not centered enough on Christ. As a result, they make life a burden. Insights drawn from the Augustinian heritage of the Protestant Reformation help us recognize how empty and unhappy such a religiously Narcissist mode of existence feels, and why we need the Law in its Theological Use to condemn sin despite our resistance to this Word.

Both Augustine and Martin Luther taught that without the condemning Word of the Law of God regarding our sin, we drive away Christ.[31] Luther contended that we don't want that Word, don't want to learn of our frailty and sickness, to feel disdain for our lives. We are like oxen tied to a yoke and pulling the Law with great toil and no reward, eventually getting slaughtered, like students who hate strict teachers.[32] We need the Law, Luther contended, because "sin is not felt while it is being committed."[33] The Reformer's words in a 1530 Easter Sermon seem as if they could have been written against Rick Warren and Prosperity Gospel preaching, especially their diminution of the doctrine of Sin. If we try to abolish sin, he contended, we are trying to displace Christ and act as if we were Christ. "Rather, let Christ remain Christ; let Him keep His office." We have enough of our own sins. Guard against imagining we can do it all.[34] Augustine and Martin Luther both understood that the less stress on the grace of God we see, in Warren and Osteen the less centered on God we are, the more on ourselves.

WHY WE SHOULDN'T WANT TO STAY WHERE WARREN LEAVES US

To remain in a state centered on oneself is to live a life filled with burdens and empty meaninglessness. We'll talk more about that in the next chapter. For now, suffice it to reiterate how the Narcissist lifestyle and the associated socioeconomic dynamics I've been considering are not a happy way to live. A life concentrated on oneself, on finding pleasure, with no continuities over time, with nothing to stand for, leaves little for which to live. Not even purpose or prosperity are very inviting if they have no ultimate significance beyond self.

St. Augustine clearly understands these observations. He spoke of human life in our sinful state as an emptiness, a falling into nothingness.[35] We are a race curious to know about the lives of others, but slothful to correct our own.[36] Loving gossip and the sensational as we do, it is hard to argue with the African Father about that point. Famed seventeenth-century French Augustinian Blaise Pascal offered an intriguing challenge to American Christianity's, Warren's, and the Prosperity Gospel progenitors' relative silence about our sinful human condition. "If our condition were truly happy," he contended, "we should not need to divert ourselves from thinking about it [as they have]."[37]

Pascal and Augustine offer penetrating observations about the meaninglessness of life in our sinful condition, a mode of existence filled with endless repetitive cycles of futility—from boredom to anxiety, from dependence to desire for independence, from adversity to prosperity and back, a life of restless tossing instability filled with storms of pride and the depths of curiosity.[38] One can hear the echoes of Ecclesiastes 1 and its testimony to the vanity of the various cycles of life and aging in such comments (biblical testimony absent in both the visions of Warren and Osteen). Our lives are so distorted and filled with the evil we would like to avoid, Augustine contends, that we begin to wink at sin, even to the point of seeing great and detestable sins as trivial.[39] One might say that the African Father has explained the dynamics of the moral breakdown so many social commentators of our day lament.

The real problem with our condition, with why the influential theologies of Warren and Prosperity Gospel preachers do not really address these dynamics, is that people do not want to admit they are sinners, and will not unless confronted with the Law and Christ as I intend to do in the next chapters. The Reformer put it this way in a commentary on Psalm 1:1. He wrote:

> And, indeed, nowadays no one wants to be a sinner any longer or to do wrong! Whence, then, the godless, and so many of them? The reason is, says the psalmist, that men call all they do, acting on sound advice, prudence, wisdom,

right, and good. . . . So things go according to the proverb:
All men are pleased with what they do. A world of fools,
I'm telling you![40]

Purpose-driven living (as well as the quest for prosperity) is
likely to nurture lives of guilt and meaninglessness. Because they
lead us to guilt or leave us with the sense of empty meaninglessness just described, these proposed worldviews fail to lift the
burden of self-centeredness. A life of brave sinning is an alternative that can free us from these burdens—free us in the sense of
conceding the meaninglessness of life I've been describing in this
chapter. Sometimes knowing your situation, no matter how bad
it is, can free you. It sets you free from the burden of thinking it
could be different, that you can make it different. Brave sinners
don't need to navel-gaze so much, asking why things aren't better
or different. The life of brave sinning Martin Luther and I are
proposing is also a life of grace turned over to God, a life that
affords you and me the unconditional love we need to have the
courage to face these realities of our condition. Ever hear of gal-
lows humor? Yes, life is hell, but let's get a drink and have some
fun. The brave sinner knows that God's forgiving grace provides
the courage we need in order to embrace and thrive in our circumstances. In order to appreciate how and why such a worldview
makes life more bearable, is fun, and even affords an opportunity
to break with American's Narcissist trends, we need to get clear
on what sin is, why we can't escape it, and why you and I need
to take it more seriously than Warren and Osteen do. It is to that
task we now turn.

An Augustinian
Re-Education about Sin

Relevant Genetic Data

If we are going to examine Martin Luther's concept of brave sinning as an alternative to the views of Rick Warren and the Prosperity Gospel, we need to be clear about the nature of sin and why we can't avoid it. This clarification is especially necessary in view of the optimism about human nature that characterizes both Western society and the fact that the most influential versions of modern Christianity have compromised the Protestant Reformation's Augustinian interpretation of human nature. And in overlooking the Augustinian appreciation that all we do is marred by sin, that we are trapped by our selfish desires, Rick Warren as well as much Prosperity Gospel preaching neglect Christianity's cutting-edge critique of our destructive contemporary social trends, and in so doing forfeit total dependence on God.

Misunderstandings abound, even in the Church, regarding the doctrine of Original Sin. In our present therapeutic/Narcissist ethos, most Americans are likely to hear the phrase "original sin" and smile uneasily. The whole idea seems rather quaint, the cultural gurus proclaim. People are not born evil as a result of the sexual origins of human life. We are self-made human beings, society contends. We determine our own fate; we must take responsibility for the good and evil we do and not make excuses with a crutch like original sin. Of course, Rick Warren reminds us, perhaps we make our mistakes. But surely we can do some good things, he and other megachurch preachers insist. Besides, society contends (saturated as it is by therapeutic jargon and values), we need to affirm human capacities and not be so negative.

I have already discussed how many pastors of different denominations report that if they refer several times to human sinfulness or if they condemn sin several Sundays in a row, someone in the congregation is likely to chide them for being too negative, for failing to build up their congregation. As much as American society as a whole, the Church is heavily ensconced in the therapeutic cultural ethos and its optimistic view of human nature. Salvation and the healthy spiritual life are about psychologically healthy existence, life without guilt. We are told, even by Joel Osteen, that people unburdened of such negativity will do the right thing.

All of these contentions, in both the contemporary church and in American society, bespeak the kind of optimism and therapeutic preoccupations we have already identified in Warren's and Osteen's thought as well as in today's prevailing social trends. They also suggest precisely the same worldview that led St. Augustine (354–430) to formulate the doctrine of Original Sin: the heresy of the English monk Pelagius.

AUGUSTINIAN AND PRE-AUGUSTINIAN ROOTS

Although Augustine was the one to formulate the doctrine of Original Sin as it eventually became codified as official Church teaching at the Council of Ephesus in 431 and again at the Synod of Orange in 529, there were significant early precedents for the doctrine. The first Christian monks who fled to African deserts in hopes of finding a way to bear Christ's Cross affirmed a strong doctrine of Sin. St. Anthony (ca. 251–356), the most famous of these monks, is a prime example. He combined this commitment, though, with an affirmation of free will.[1] His colleagues in the desert were more radical in speaking of the hold sin has on us. Longinus and Matoes spoke of sin in terms of passions that overcome the soul. Moses the Negro found the image to describe the sins that gripped him, noting that "sins run behind me, and I do not see them. . . ." Earlier in the third century, a Bishop in North Africa, Commodianus, had even identified sin with desire.[2] The great champion of the Trinitarian doctrine, Athanasius (ca. 296–373), Bishop of Alexandria, an older contemporary of Augustine who was himself a devoted advocate of the monks, continued in their tradition regarding the seriousness with which he took human sin. He spoke of the corruption caused by sin. On account of such sin, he contended, the human race was perishing and the image of God disappearing in human beings as they became clouded by demoniacal deceit and insatiable in sinning. Like the monks, though, Athanasius still affirmed human free will.[3]

Earlier eminent theologians made comments suggestive of the doctrine of Original Sin. Tertullian (ca.160–225) referred to Adam as "the originator of our race and our sin." Cyprian of Carthage (200–258) subsequently made affirmations about Baptism that were also directly pertinent to the development of the doctrine of original sin. In justifying the practice of infant baptism, he referred to the sin of infants in the sense of their having been "born of the flesh according to Adam," contracting "the contagion of the ancient death."[4] These early theologians laid significant groundwork for understanding sin as something bigger than us and our misdeeds, as a reality or condition that infects our entire nature, even from birth.

Biblical Roots

Of course there were biblical precedents for these affirmations. The Old Testament has many express references to "sins" against the Commandments and the Law of God, and the Gospels continued to refer to sins in this tradition. At an early stage in the development of these Old Testament texts sin came to be related not just to misdeeds but also to a lack of faith (Exodus 32, esp. v. 21).

The Genesis 3 account of the Fall of Adam and Eve became a crucial text for the Christian doctrine of Sin. Although Jewish leaders did not understand the Fall in this way, New Testament writers began to speak of the transmission of sin to all humanity through Adam (Romans 5:12–14; 1 Corinthians 15:22). Psalm 51:5 ("I was . . . a sinner when my mother conceived me") can be cited to support this idea that one is born in sin by virtue of the Fall.

Other texts are pertinent for establishing the pervasive character of sin, that it is more than mere misdeeds and is instead a reality that saturates the whole of human nature. Romans 7 (esp. vv. 14–23) portrays sin as a reality that forces human beings to do and to will what they otherwise would not want to. Ecclesiastes 4:4 also seems relevant. The text reads: "Then I saw that all labor and all skill in work come from one person's envy of another. This also is vanity and a striving after wind." The text suggests that every dimension of human activity is the result of envy and the desire to get ahead of one's neighbor (i.e., the result of competition and concupiscence).

The Augustinian Synthesis

The occasion for gathering up these insights into a fully developed doctrine of Original Sin in which all sins are said to be rooted was a famous controversy between Augustine and Pelagius (ca. 360–420), a devout monk from Britain (perhaps Ireland). Fervently pious, the monk despaired over the lukewarm Christianity that seemed to plague his contemporaries. His response was to teach and preach a rigid moralism. Christian life in Pelagius' view was all about the effort to overcome sins in order to attain salvation. This required a belief that people have complete freedom to choose whether to sin or not to sin.

Pelagius' debate with Augustine was occasioned by the African Father's prayer in his classic work *The Confessions*: "Give what Thou command and command what Thou wilt." Pelagius rejected the idea that God commands the impossible, as Augustine seemed to imply.[5] The two contemporaries would be locked in a heated debate for years, with Augustine's side eventually prevailing.

The African Father's primary agenda was not to lament the power of sin, but to assert the primacy of God's action and forgiving love, to confess that Christ is humanity's only hope. Pelagius' portrait of how we are saved contradicted this Augustinian vision. If we are not totally immersed in sin, then it logically follows that we can save ourselves, that we do not need Christ. The testimony of Mark 2:7 that God alone can forgive sins, and that only Jesus has been able to exercise that authority, seems to be at stake here.

In addition to these commitments, Augustine's own life had revealed to him the hopelessness of the human condition in sin.[6] So bound to sin are we, he insisted (in the spirit of Romans 7), that when it comes to avoiding sin we have no free will. Without grace, we cannot stop sinning. As he puts it: "Free choice alone, if the way of truth is hidden, avails for nothing but sin; and when the right action and true aim has begun to appear clearly, there is still no doing, no devotion, no good life . . ."[7]

If we have free will and can in principle choose the good, we open the door again to the possibility that we can overcome sin and save ourselves. Again our total dependence on God is at stake in these commitments. (For Christians, certain biblical texts such as Romans 3:21–28, Galatians 3:1–14, and Ephesians 2:8–9 are on the line.) The next time you are tempted to raise questions about the doctrine of Sin or want to affirm free will (in the sense of asserting that we have the power to do good without grace), you might keep in mind that in so doing you effectively minimize our dependence on God. As I've been suggesting, this is one of the major problems with Warren and Osteen.

Our bondage to sin does not necessarily mean that we are reduced to robots. It is theologically appropriate to continue to assert our freedom to choose actions without compromising the claim that we are in bondage to sin. For example, you, the reader, are free to decide whether to continue reading this book today or whether to discontinue reading. On Augustine's grounds, and most compatible with findings of modern research on the brain, either way you are sinning, because the decision you made in each case is self-serving (doing what makes you feel good).[8]

Martin Luther also described this inescapability of sin in all we do with the Latin phrase *in curvatus in se* (curved in on ourselves). As he put it prior to the Reformation:

> The reason is that our nature has been so deeply curved in upon itself because of the viciousness of original sin that it not only turns the finest gifts of God in upon itself and enjoys them (as is evident in the case of legalists and hypocrites), indeed, it even uses God Himself to achieve these aims, but it also seems to be ignorant of the very fact, that in acting so iniquitously, so perversely, and in such a depraved way, it is even seeking God for its own sake.[9]

As the Reformer put it elsewhere, after the onset of the Reform, we even begin to use God as a meal ticket.[10]

Sin as Concupiscence: Reformation Appropriations

The next challenge faced by Augustine was how unequivocally to assert our bondage to sin. The weight of precedent and how the biblical witness had been interpreted in previous centuries moved the African Father to talk about sin as something we are born with and to depict it in terms of desire or lust.[11] Certainly, when someone is lusting (be it a sexual lust or a lust for power or things), that person is in bondage to that person or thing. You cannot make many free decisions in the heat of passion. You just do what the lust demands.

Augustine described this bondage to lust as concupiscence, designating it as "the law of sin."[12] *Concupiscence*, of course, is a term referring to a strong compelling desire, especially like sexual lust. The term had autobiographical significance for Augustine insofar as he had struggled with sexual lust in the course of his spiritual pilgrimage. By employing the term to describe the essence of Sin, the African Father was provided with a powerful way of expressing the bondage of sin without reducing fallen humanity to the status of mere robots. Just as one cannot stop a sexual encounter in the heat of passion, so sinners seeking their own gratification cannot stop seeking it, even when they know better. It is as Paul said in Romans 7:15 and 19: "I do not understand my own actions. For I do not do what I want, but I do the very thing I hate. . . . For I do not do the good I want, but the evil I do not want is what I do."

Augustine conceives of fallen human beings as addicts. Like sex addicts, the more we are driven to seek pleasure and self-fulfillment, the less we will be satisfied, and so the more pleasures we will need to seek. The more you desire, the more you sin, and the more you sin, the more you desire. The African Father more or less made this point when he claimed that (human) nature and custom (or actions) join together to render cupidity stronger. Both Martin Luther and John Calvin, admirers of Augustine, also described Sin in terms of concupiscence.[13]

It would be a mistake to understand Augustine as defining Sin merely as lustful action that results in visible violations of the Ten Commandments and of the expectations of good citizenship in a society. His point in describing Sin as concupiscence was to make clear that *all* human deeds, even those outwardly good, are sinful. Augustine did believe sinful human beings are capable of outwardly good deeds. Indeed, such acts are no less outwardly good than deeds motivated by the love of God. He even claimed that the words of pride (concupiscence) are akin to those of love. Both can feed the hungry and care for the dying. The difference is that love does what it does for Christ, while pride does what it does in order that the doer may be glorified.[14]

In developing this theme of sin as concupiscence, Martin Luther made similar points, both prior to and soon after the outbreak of the Reformation:

> For man cannot be seeking his own advantages and love himself above all things. And this is the sum of all his iniquities. Hence even in good things and virtues men seek themselves, that is, they seek to please themselves and applaud themselves. . . . I say now that no one should doubt that all our good works are mortal sins, if they are judged according to God's judgment and severity and not accepted as good by grace alone.[15]

For Luther, even our best deeds are sins. This is also what John Calvin meant in implying that human beings are totally depraved.[16]

There is no ridding ourselves of sin on these grounds. Martin Luther spoke of sin as a fine cat who beguiles us. It is like a man's beard, he claimed, of which we can never rid ourselves:

> The original sin in a man is like his beard, which, though shaved off today so that a man is very smooth around his mouth, yet grows again by tomorrow morning. As long as a man is alive, such growth of the hair and the beard does not stop. But when the shovel beats the ground on his grave, it stops. Just so original sin remains in us and bestirs itself as long as we live . . .[17]

There is a sense in which on these Augustinian grounds the behavior of Mother Teresa and Martin Luther King Jr. was not better than that of Hitler or Osama bin Laden. All were driven in some sense by lust for power and influence (concupiscence). Before God, they and we stand equally condemned unless the miracle of God's forgiving grace intervenes. However, if we speak in terms of relative degrees of human goodness and justice, then of course the actions of King and Teresa may be judged as better, even as good. Augustine himself made this distinction as he spoke of a "righteousness in the Law" which is mere obedience to its letter, as distinct from the "righteousness of the Law" which only God gives by grace. Some Reformation-era heirs of the African Father, notably Martin Luther, offered a similar distinction between the "civic or external righteousness" of the good citizen and the righteousness of God given in justification of the sinner.[18]

Everything that fallen human beings do is ultimately driven not by the love of God, but by the burning desire to please the ego. Thus Augustine and Martin Luther claimed that new desires (concupiscence) are increased and receive greater energies from prohibitions of the Law.[19] When I am urged to do something to succeed, become powerful, do good, my ego begins to crave these things even more than ever before. As a result, even the good deeds that I do are scarred by my egocentric desires to do good.

The Law of God energizes concupiscence in other ways. Prohibitions have a way of causing rebellion, at least of the covert sort. When someone says "do it my way or else" or that you cannot undertake a certain activity, it is likely you will want to do that forbidden deed even more. In our sinful condition, we never outgrow our childishness. We are like children who are forbidden certain toys or like teenagers wanting more "freedom." The prohibitions of God's Law make us want what is forbidden even more. The Law is indeed the curse St. Paul said it was in Galatians 3:10–14.

Augustine found another provocative way to express the insidious character of human behavior after the Fall into sin. He began with the reflection that of all that exists only God can be enjoyed, for only God gives the good and happy life. All other things are there only for use, since they in themselves cannot offer the good and happy life. In short, the best we can do in our interactions with the things of the world is to use them. Is that not true? Ultimately, do we not *use* what we love—our vocations, our friends, even our families—to our own benefit and for our own gratification? Augustine concedes that there is a way of finding true joy in the things of the earth, but only when we enjoy these loves as things or vehicles of God, who alone brings true joy.[20] Even in these cases, though, Christians are still only using the things of the earth, only using the people they love. In using loved ones as vehicles to find joy, people seem to subordinate them to their own desires and ego. On this side of eternity, then, concupiscence never goes away.

These reflections help us understand what a life without concupiscence, a life lived in eternity or before the Fall into sin, is like. It would be a life of enjoyment, not one of using people and things. We need to clarify this, or it is hard to understand these realities in a meaningful way. I will not elaborate much on this point here, since this is the topic for another time.[21] But it should be noted here that there is an increasing openness among genetic researchers to acknowledging that all human beings may be descended from a common African mother, insofar as we all share a remarkably similar configuration of mitochondrial DNA (structures inside all human cells), which is inherited from our mothers. At this point, suffice it to say that if we could construe the original creation as a state of fully enjoying God, then all that would surround us would be enjoyed as stemming from Him. In such a state I and all that surrounds me may be enjoyed because it is of God. We must all share a common gene pool, as it were, a restoration of the common gene pool in which human life began in Eve's womb.[22] Consequently, my desires are no longer concupiscent, just for personal fulfillment, but for the fulfillment of the genes outside me, for my neighbor. It is as good if they succeed as if I do. Although some expressions of human relations may foreshadow this reality (like the love of parent for a child or between the love between spouses), since the Fall into sin none succeeds in canceling out my prioritizing of my own needs over those of my kin.

Augustine made his point regarding the inescapable character of concupiscence and egocentricity in a way that has been most controversial. However, when we really analyze the point in light of the realities of the sex drive, it seems valid. Essentially, Augustine concluded that we are born into our concupiscence. Following the lead of an earlier North African Bishop Cyprian of Carthage, he maintained that we are concupiscent because we are conceived in concupiscence.[23]

Augustine's point is not to suggest anything so simplistic as that we are conceived in sin, or that sex is sinful. But the reality is that the "very embrace [between spouses] which is lawful and honorable cannot be effected without the ardour of lust." Likewise, the sexual encounter that follows from such foreplay is driven by concupiscence and lust. (If you do not have some of that left in a marital encounter, it may not be a good marriage.) Sometimes the result of this encounter is fertilization of the egg, the beginning of human life. And so God uses human concupiscence to create new life. The product of such human concupiscence is likely to be marked by its concupiscent parental origins, just as we bear our parents' genes. Conceived as the product of concupiscence, it is no wonder we turn out that way.

A distinct twentieth-century version of this way of thinking can be articulated on the basis of the work of the eminent Swiss Reformed theologian Karl Barth. In essence, he maintained the doctrine of Original Sin, the inevitability of sin, by contending that we are what we do or what is done to us. Human beings do not have static, essential natures. For example, Mark Ellingsen is nothing more that the sum total of all the things he has done and have happened to him. Given the Barthian scheme, we can observe that just as Mark Ellingsen and the readers of this volume have been exposed only to concupiscent human beings (except for Jesus Christ), it is hardly surprising that the nature formed by encounter with the world would itself be concupiscent.[24] We can understand Augustine's depiction of original sin in light of Barth's more socio-logical analysis. Either way, the inevitability of sin, the assertion of how we are marred by sin from birth, is non-negotiable for the classic Christian doctrine of Sin.

Augustine and those who followed him (especially the Protestant Reformers) sought to protect these non-negotiable assertions by insisting that even Christians always remain concupiscent. Concupiscence remains even after one comes to faith and is bap-tized. Indeed the African Father expressly claimed that sin is not removed in Baptism, just no longer imputed. Martin Luther, in particular, made this point clear with his concept of the Christian as *simul iustus et peccator* (fully saint, but also fully sinner). We have already noted his concept of Sin as something like a man's beard that you can shave but never fully eradicate.[25] If this were not true, Christians would not need Christ and grace as much as they did before conversion.

Many contemporary Christians and even some denomina-tions (especially Methodist-Holiness churches, which only refer to our "inclination" to sin) have difficulties with this idea. But if Augustine's and the Protestant Reformers' formulation of the doc-trine of Original Sin are taken seriously, then Christians must con-cede the insidious egoism of which they cannot rid themselves. Even going to church, participating in its activities, preaching a sermon, and prayer are undertaken for one's own enrichment or (at least in some subcultures and communities) for the acclaim or appreciation such activities furnish, as much as they are done for God.

I hasten to note that references to Augustine's views in this chap-ter represent a constructive appropriation of the African Father's thinking, more than a historical-critical analysis. As the exposi-tion has made clear, the version of Augustine I have portrayed is more in line with Protestant appropriations of his thought, which consistently identify concupiscence with sin. In fact, the historical Augustine sometimes rejected the equation of concupiscence with sin.[26] But this is a book proposing Reformation appropriations of the Augustinian heritage as a way of addressing problems inherent in the theology of Rick Warren and in our present American (as well as Western) social ethos. Besides, as we'll now observe, the strand of Augustine equating concupiscence with sin seems most compatible with cutting-edge Biochemistry.

BIOCHEMISTRY, GENETICS, AND ORIGINAL SIN

Genetic research indicates that genes play a significant role in making human beings who they are. Human bodies, it seems, function to maximize reproduction of DNA. As a result, because of the genes' struggle to survive, universal love and welfare of the species as a whole do not make evolutionary sense. These dynamics have led researcher Richard Dawkins to refer to the "selfish gene."[27] His theorizing certainly explains kin selection—why parents love their children and why members of ethnic groups tend to prefer their own and guard each other's welfare over outsiders. These Genealogical insights clearly endorse the Augustinian-Pauline concept of sin as an egocentricity that underlies all that we do, even the very best of our actions.

However, the scientific guild has sensed the difficulties in accounting for meaningful social existence if human relationships are ultimately a matter of egocentric kin selection. One theory that has sought to deal with the problem has been the theory of Sociobiology, first developed by Edward O. Wilson. According to this scheme, genetic evolution has brought human beings to the point where they are dependent on culture in order to flourish and survive. The learned behaviors and enforced cooperation cultures make possible are in the interests of human genes, because humans intuitively know their genes will be proliferated maximally through such cooperation.[28] Society or culture in turn enforces altruism, behavior that increases fitness of the other even at one's own expense.

The "altruistic" behavior that emerges from these genetic drives is not truly altruistic (not a manifestation of a self-emptying agape love). It is in fact driven by the self-love or selfishness of the genes, either by their own biological drive to love themselves (love for one's kin in whom one's genes are to be found, is a genetic self-love) or by the drive to have more opportunities to diversify the gene pool (which is only possible in the context of an ordered society).

Another related dynamic pertains to the propensity of our genes not to cooperate with or be altruistic to those who do not share our genes (those to whom we are not related). Biocultural analysis regards it as society's function to enforce cooperation in these cases. Much in line with Augustinian thinking, society is understood as functioning to enforce civil, moral behavior when our genetic makeup predisposes us to conflict with those who do not share our genes.

True enough, some interpreters have contended that this genetic and biological data actually challenge the doctrine of Original Sin, precisely because they seem to imply that it is "natural." My response is that what science regards as natural is a post-Fall reality, not necessarily identical with the way in which God intended the cosmos. As I noted previously, we can see how these mechanisms would not necessarily entail a concupiscent, sinful condition if we posit an original creation and vision of eternity in which all human beings sense that they share a common gene pool (given in our common mother and in Christ), such that our desires are no longer only about me and my immediate kin, but equally for the sake of all (since I share a common gene pool with all).[29]

In chapter five we will see more fully that no less than Sociobiology and Genetics, cutting-edge Neurobiology also indicates that even spirituality and love have a selfish (sinful) dimension. In both heterosexual love as well as in prayer and worship, it seems, pleasurable neurochemicals that ferry signals from one brain neuron to another are secreted. This data provides further testimony to the fact that on this side of the Fall, human beings are sinful and selfish in all they do. Augustine's reading of Paul and the Protestant Reformers, not Warren and Osteen, are right about human nature!

It might be good Science, but the idea that we are looking out for our own interests in all we do goes against the grain of much American (certainly Enlightenment) optimism about human nature. But if you are bold enough to be honest, is it not true that you and I have never done a truly selfless deed, that even the apparent acts of altruism were at least subliminally motivated by the positive feelings or enhanced status we received for such deeds? Be honest: To deny these biblically, scientifically, experientially verified realities is an act of self-seeking cowardice on our parts.

Because of our concupiscence, our innate propensity to use people and position for our own benefit, all our social interactions will always be flawed. As I have noted, no relationship, not even with one's beloved family, will be perfect, free of hassles and heartaches, for even these relationships are marred by power struggles between members to get their own way. Get real about love, community engagement, even spirituality. A life of brave sinning, which I will next consider, gives us permission to admit these flaws and joyfully revel in what's good about what we have, despite the times when one party gets his or her way through manipulation. Christians may even enjoy their imperfect relationships when family and friends, when community members are seen as gifts and vehicles of God, and precautions are taken to guard against one-sided dominance of the interests of some in the family over those of the others. In the next chapters we begin to learn how and why that can happen, why such a life of brave sinning feels so joyful and good.

An Introduction to
Brave Sinning

A God-Centered Life

This book will send a lot of wrong messages unless we are very clear about Martin Luther's concept of "*brave sinning*" (*pecca fortiter*). The Reformer and I are not teaching permission "to do your own thing." Rather, the concept "sin bravely" is a word of permission to do God's "thing" joyously and with reckless abandon.

I began to clarify this concept in the introduction. As noted, brave sinning has to do with a courageous trust in God as well as a bold awareness and willingness to confess what I reviewed in the preceding chapter—that in everything we do (even in our apparently good and noble activities) we are sinning. Such bold sinning gets the focus off the person and on to God who, the brave sinner boldly confesses, affirms sinners. This focus on God includes the awareness by brave sinners that because they can do no good, any good that happens in their lives must be God's work despite their seedy motives. This has the salubrious effect of leading to joy and happiness, since the pressure is now removed to do good and be good.

Brave sinning gets the focus on God in other ways. Brave sinners, aware that sin permeates all that transpires, recognize the meaningless, chaotic character of life. Such an awareness, coupled with faith in God, also leads to a self-forgetfulness about one's circumstances, which in turn leads to happiness. There is a compatibility here with the Puritan Confessions in their *Shorter Catechism*, that the purpose of life (our chief end) is to glorify God and enjoy him forever.[1] As the Puritans recognized a correlation between happiness and being centered on God, so we will see Martin Luther and modern Neurobiological research teach us that you are happier when you forget yourself and concentrate on God. First, though, we need to clarify Martin Luther's reflections on this exciting, but easily misunderstood way to live.

EVOLUTION OF THE CONCEPT

We have already emphasized that one cannot understand Martin Luther's concept of brave sinning apart from his conviction that we sin in all we do. Correspondingly, this entails a God-centeredness in Luther, a commitment to affirming justification by grace though faith at all costs. The Reformer wrote:

> For the issue here is nothing trivial for Paul; it is the principal doctrine of Christianity. When this is recognized and held before one's eyes, everything else seems vile and worthless, For what is Peter? What is Paul? What is an angel of heaven? What is all creation in comparison with the doctrine of justification?[2]

Because I can be confident of God's love for me, "come hell or high water" (and of course brave sinners know it's mostly hell on this side of the End of Time), I can live with myself and my situation, not get so bent out of shape about it. I don't get so burned out when I'm not fretting about being burned out. Deadlines, chaos, even loneliness aren't as bad when I'm not worried about how bad it is to live through such experiences. The great American Reformed theologian of the last century Reinhold Niebuhr characterized Luther's concept of brave sinning as nothing more than a realistic cynicism that leads to healthy rejoicing. He described brave sinning this way:

> This means, don't be so morbid about the fact that you're selfish; don't deny that you are self-regarding, but work in life and hope that by grace—this perhaps is the door to the real answer—you will be redeemed. *By grace.*[3]

Luther's actual references to brave sinning seem to warrant Niebuhr's analysis.

Probably the best-known occasion in which Luther wrote about brave sinning was in his 1521 *Letter to Philip Melanchthon.* The Reformer was corresponding with his primary intellectual ally, perhaps the leading intellectual of the movement. Luther had been in exile, and in his absence from Wittenberg another of his colleagues at the university, a more radical Reformer named Andreas Bodenstein von Karlstadt (ca. 1480–1541), had sought to abolish all sorts of Roman Catholic practices by means of a strict moralism. Such legalism went against the grain of Luther's thinking, and so in response he wrote to encourage Melanchthon boldly to resist both Karlstadt's and the Catholic Church's quest for purity without sin. It's not a problem, he advised Melanchthon, if Christians get themselves soiled with sin or engage certain Catholic activities that Karlstadt disapproved. In fact such boldness nourishes faith:

> If you are a preacher of grace, then preach a true and not a fictitious grace; if grace is true, you must bear a true and not a fictitious sin. God does not save people who are only

> pretended sinners. Be a sinner and sin bravely, but believe
> and rejoice in Christ even more bravely, for He is victorious
> over sin, death, and the world. As long as we are here [in
> this world] we have to sin. . . . No sin will separate us from
> the Lamb. . . . Pray boldly—you too are a mighty sinner.[4]

We are not to deny sin, but bravely to confess our sinfulness, for
it gives us confidence to know that we are totally dependent of
Christ who has won the victory and from whom we can never
be separated.

Most Luther Scholarship fails to appreciate that there were
other occasions when the Reformer spoke of sinning bravely.
Because the scholarship has been so sparse on this point, we need
to examine his utterances on the matter with some care. In a sermon on Luke 18:9–14, contrasting the pharisaic self-righteousness
of many Christians with the willingness of the faithful tax collector
to confess their sins, Luther noted again the wonderful confidence
and dependence on God that comes with a brave willingness to
confess that one is a sinner. He wrote:

> 43. Therefore see to it, that you properly follow this tax
> collector, and become like him. Namely, in the first place,
> that you be not a false but a real sinner; not only in words
> but in reality and from the heart acknowledge yourself
> worthy before God of His wrath and eternal punishment,
> and bring before Him in truth these words, "me a poor
> sinner"; but in the same flight lay hold of the other words:
> "Be Thou merciful to me. . . ."[5]

Note how false (cowardly) sinners are unwilling to concede that
they are sinners; they are too preoccupied with what the self can
accomplish. In the famed 1518 Heidelberg Disputation, in which

Luther was called on by his Augustinian Order and the Pope to defend his theology, the budding Reformer made similar points:

> Thus it is that those people say, "God does not demand perfection," whereas they should say, "God pardons." But whom? Those who feel secure and those who do not believe that they sin? Not at all. Rather He pardons those who say, "Forgive us our sins," those who recognize and hate their wickedness with a true heart. . . . Therefore, it is the sweetest righteousness of God the Father that He does not save imaginary, but rather real sinners, sustaining us in spite of our sins and accepting works and our lives which are all deserving of rejection until He perfects and saves us.[6]

The pressure is off to achieve. The sinner is affirmed. There is a wonderful freedom and joy, along with a realism about the fallibility and self-centeredness of human life, which are also entailed by these insights for Luther. Invoking the concept of brave sinning once again while eating a meal with students and other houseguests (his Table Talk), Luther is reported to have contended that we need never despair because we are great sinners:

> We should not become despondent or despair because of our sin and because we are great sinners; for God has caused the forgiveness of sins to be publicly proclaimed to all who honestly recognize and confess their sins and to be offered to everybody, no one excluded. Nor will He change His mind.[7]

The theme of brave sinning conjures feelings of hope and comfort. Being a sinner does not stop you from being a Christian. In fact, the Gospel of Jesus Christ is not about making people better or even more faithful. Being a Christian is about getting something (from Christ). Luther made that point stunningly in a sermon in his *Church Postil.* He wrote:

> To make good people does not belong to the Gospel, for it only makes Christians. It takes much more to be a Christian than to be pious. A person can easily be pious, but not a Christian. A Christian knows nothing to say about his piety, for he finds in himself nothing good or pious. . . . So one is not called a Christian because he does much, but because he receives something from Christ, draws from him and lets Christ only give to him.[8]

Again we are reminded how brave sinning helps us get our priorities right. The awareness that we sin in everything we do takes the focus off our actions, off our contributions to living as Christians, and instead refocuses us back on what Christ has done for us. Brave sinners live with a tension between being self-centered and God-centered, between being 100 percent a sinner and 100 percent a fully forgiven saint of God (*simul iustus et peccator*).[9] In that sense they are both "in" the world, but not "of" the world (Galatians 6:14; 1 Corinthians 7:30). As such, brave sinners both share in the self-seeking narcissist ethos of our time while also getting away from it with their God-centeredness.

FREEDOM FROM THE LAW: BRAVE SINNERS STILL DO GOOD WORKS

True enough, the life of brave sinning is a life of freedom from the Law of God (Galatians 3:10–14). But I have already tried to make the case that the concept of sinning bravely does not offer permission to "do your own thing." That is cowardly sinning—a narcissistic preoccupation with who one is. I need to clarify first what Martin Luther, Augustine, and St. Paul mean by freedom from the Law.

In all cases such freedom means that I need not depend on God's Law for guidance about how to live as a Christian. Nor do I require the exhortation of the Decalogue or distinct Bible teachings in order to have the motivation I need to do good. Although it was by no means his only position on good works, Augustine, in his *Ten Homilies on the Epistle of John to the Parthians*, claimed that Christians are to "love, and do whatever [they] will."[10]

Just as the African Father's and Paul's remarks seem to imply not just that good works undertaken by Christians are spontaneous but also that ethics are situational, so Martin Luther seems to endorse this perspective, quite expressly. In a treatise devoted to the subject of good works the Reformer compared the relationship Christians have with Christ to a good relationship among happily married spouses. Clearly in a good relationship rules are not necessary; the couple seems to know intuitively what to do to and for each other. Luther wrote:

> It further follows from this that a Christian man living in this faith has no need of a teacher of good works; he does whatever the occasion calls for, and all is done well. . . . We may see this is an everyday example. When a husband and wife really love one another, have pleasure in each other, and thoroughly believe in their love, who teaches them how they are to behave one to another, what they are to do or not to do, say or not to say, what they are to think? Confidence alone teaches them all this, and even more than is necessary. For such a man there is no distinction of works. He does the great and the important as gladly as the small and unimportant and vice versa. Moreover, he does them all as a free man with a glad, peaceful, and confident heart.[11]

Notice that for Luther, one work is like another. One is not more important or more spiritual than another. Taking out the garbage for one's family is as great a work as community organizing, as spiritual a work as prayer and preaching. This fits the concept of the priesthood of all believers.[12]

As Luther affirms in the preceding quotation that Christians have no need for the Law of God to teach good works, the logical consequence is that the Christian life of freedom from the Law and brave sinning may involve violating the Law of God. Late in his career Luther wrote:

> Thus in their wars the saints frequently deceived their enemies, but those are lies one is permitted to use in the service of God against the devil and the enemies of God.[13]

It is useful to expound further in the quotation from his sermons on 1 John on the Reformer's comparison of the Christian's relation to God in Christ to the relation between spouses in a good marriage. Recent cutting-edge scholarship undertaken by some Finnish Lutherans has sought to emphasize that something like this image is characteristically employed by the Reformer in order to express the doctrine of Justification. Certainly Luther frequently referred to justification by grace as a "blessed exchange," noting that just as in a marriage (in the days before prenuptial agreements) the couple shares all property, so the believer and Christ share all things in common. His righteousness and goodness become ours in a derivative way. St. Augustine also at least at times spoke about Justification this way. Sharing in Christ's righteousness, the sinner is then also a saint (*simultaneously saint and sinner*, to use Luther's phrase).[14] In fact in the 1520 treatise on good works cited above in which he used the marriage analogy to describe why despite our sin we can't help but do good when we are caught up in Christ, the Reformer observed the way in which Christ's work changes the brave sinner's heart:

If you see in the crucified Christ that God is so kindly disposed toward you that He even gives His own Son for you, then your heart in turn must grow sweet and disposed toward God.[15]

There can be little dispute that Luther's and Augustine's image of justification as a union with Christ (akin to a marriage with him) takes good works seriously, makes them a necessary part of the Christian life. In fact Jesus, the man of love and good works, combined these two elements with brave sinning, as Luther reminds us that Christ himself was the greatest of all sinners. The Reformer wrote:

And all the proponents saw this, that Christ was to become the greatest thief, murderer, adulterer, robber, desecrator, blasphemer, etc. there has ever been anywhere in the world.[16]

It is hardly surprising that we would take up Christ's tasks of bearing burdens of others joyfully. In a good marriage, when you share a common family legacy, all sorts of good, warm, and loving things happen among the partners and family members. Sometimes, maybe even often, these deeds are done with joy and bring pleasure. No one makes you do those loving things. There is no pressure in these relationships. The relationship does not depend on such deeds; it is based on love. Has that not been your experience?

This image also has implications for addressing Narcissism. Recall that the narcissist is empty. The Christian, on Luther's grounds, is full (filled with Christ), and so less in need of acclaim and self-promotion in order to fill the emptiness.[17] Friendship (especially our relationship with Christ) fills us.

Although neither Luther nor Augustine elaborated on this point, the reliance on the image of a marital-like union of the believer with Christ nicely serves their joint contention that Christians, though righteous in Christ, ever remain sinners, and expressly Luther's notion of the Christian as a brave sinner. Certainly concupiscence (and so sin) is evident in good marriages, even in the most loving interactions of couples, on the side of the Fall (even in our marriage to Jesus). We get lots of pleasures from our spouses.

LIFE IS ABSURD: LIFE AS PLAY

Because we sin in everything we do, we should not take life so seriously. The concept of brave sinning teaches us to accept the fact that sin renders all our important projects nothing more than child's play. The big business deal, the big house, the latest sensual pleasure, and the big book we are writing will not last forever. In most cases, they won't even last very long.

Augustine, the formulator of Original Sin, made this point in a negative way to indicate how absurd all our adult business and political activities are. The idling boys do is rather like the idling grownups do on their jobs. In other words, what we do on the job is not very important, just a way of killing time and having fun.[18]

We could take this point to help us recognize that we make too much of our adult undertakings and let it set us free from pressure. If the job and other adult activities are like the games youth play, then like child's play these activities are there to be enjoyed. How interesting and freeing to think that important activities like counseling, parenting, and love-making are marred by sin, just joyful games, through which God in his goodness might still make something good. To look at life in terms of sin, to confess this reality bravely, can set you and me free from a lot of burn-out and pressure. At best, we are nothing more than "the hands of God" in doing good works for others in these activities, for only God could make something good out of our sinful deeds.

Of course to contend that we sin in everything we do, even in our good deeds, that all our "important" work is nothing but play, is to reduce life to absurdity. The doctrine of Sin, when boldly confessed, implies this conclusion. It entails that all we do is flawed, that the very best we ever do is finite, limited, and driven by our self-centered desires. Ecclesiastes 1:2,14. The cycles of life continue with no meaning—birth, death, more births, more deaths, with no end to the cycles. And the meaningless cycles rob us—of energy, youth, good looks, brain power, and even of the most significant loves of our lives. We dream of peace and an end to poverty, but war, exploitation, government manipulation, crime, sloth, evil, and inhumanity to our fellow human beings plague us as much as ever and will never come to an end. You and I could do all the right things in life, create higher standards of living and a more just society, and our children still might suffer want or undo all the good we have done. For all our talk of freedom, we are really just puppets of the forces of history, pushed into certain behaviors and values by society or by the crowd. Indeed, society and its various historic media have even shaped our self-image and goals, dictated what our appropriate behavior patterns should be. (Consider how society has defined the "appropriate" roles for women, minorities, and even what constitutes seemly male behavior.) In a world in which all values are relative to the individual, even proponents of liberation do little more than aim to substitute one form of oppression for another. And then the forces of nature (storms, earthquakes, droughts) are always on the horizon to threaten life itself.

Nothing seems to matter in face of such nihilism. There are no objective values, no right or wrong. Without values, impatient with limits, we have been driven to live lives of inhuman excess. But all that we have never satisfies. What we do is not really what we want. And most of the time what we think we want (especially the goods we accumulate) is not what we really want, but is what society and the media convince us to want. We have forgotten how to love life. And it does not matter sometimes it seems: Striving for excellence or passion for what we hold dear is not necessarily rewarded, and may even be derided as unhealthy or threatening to the many therapeutically saturated Americans we encounter today, narcissistically imprisoned in their mediocrity as they are yet feeling entitled to admiration. It is all so wearisome sometimes.

All our accomplishments are so minute; our most significant relationships are so fragile and will ultimately end in separation (even if it is the separation of death). And nothing we do, not even our lives, will be long remembered. Suicide seems the only logical option left. It is as my rebellious, life-affirming mother used to say during my childhood as we strolled through cemeteries in which the family elders were laid, and she noted a grave not well kept. "Oh Mark," she would utter, "think of these people. Once they were loved; now nobody cares." Cowardly sinning, optimistic Americans like Warren, Osteen, and the thousands who resonate with their visions do not want to be reminded of what Fallen human life is really like. It takes the courage that brave sinners have only through their reliance on grace to face these stark realities.

The French Existentialist philosopher Albert Camus (1913–1960), though himself an atheist, not only had a real feel for the human condition as the Augustinian vision of Christianity portrays it. (I confess that it was through reading his great book *The Rebel* that I truly first came to understand all this talk about the Fall that the Church had taught me.) His vision of life as rebellion as the only viable option for a life of order in the midst of the chaos of life has a lot in common with the Christian vision of brave sinning I've been describing.[19]

For Camus, to be a rebel is to commit oneself to the absurd dialogue between human beings asking "why" and the seemingly uncompromising meaninglessness of the universe. The rebel refuses to be what he or she is (and also to let the world be what it is), for rebels reject the adolescent furies of our age.[20] In this unwillingness to let the world be as it is, we can hear echoes of Martin Luther's Theology of the Cross. A key principle of this set of commitments (clearly related to the concept of brave sinning) is the idea that what seems attractive to us is in fact sin, while the things of God are not visible.[21] God's ways are not the way the world is now.

The difference between Camus' vision of a life of rebellion and brave sinning is that he underestimated the courage it would take to be a rebel. You and I (ordinary mortal human beings) do not possess that sort of courage and boldness. It is grace and confidence in grace that alone can provide the boldness we need to rebel. Luther put it this way in one of the prefaces to his translation of the Bible:

> Faith is a loving, daring confidence in God's grace, so sure and certain that the believer would stake his life on it a thousand times. This knowledge of and confidence in God's grace makes men glad and bold and happy in dealing with God and with all creatures.[22]

Knowledge of and confidence in God's grace makes us glad and bold in dealing with God and all creatures. Keep in mind Luther's comment about how grace not only makes us bold—it also makes us happy. Hardly surprising: If grace gives us courage to see the absurdity of life, to regard it as mired in sin such that at best life is nothing but a game, then life becomes more fun when construed as a game. We'll return to this point shortly. But first let's talk a little more about Camus' vision of the life of a rebel, as it sheds more light on brave sinning.

Camus is clear that the essence of rebellion is a protest against evil. Suffering and evil cannot be justified by the rebel.[23] Likewise brave sinners protest the evil and death to which their sin condemns them, and are audacious enough to do good anyway. They do not accept what is the case. Like Camus' rebel, brave sinners say "no," but with a refusal that does not imply renunciation. Like the rebel, brave sinners "confront an order of things which oppress."[24]

For the eminent Existentialist, echoing Christian overtones, rebellion cannot exist without a strange form of love. If all are not saved, he contends, what good is the salvation of only one? There is a generosity in rebellion, Camus suggests. In rejecting injustice, the rebel insists that everything possessed must be distributed to life and to all who live. In a comment with deep implications for the social implications in our context of the way in which rebellious brave sinning can make a difference, Camus defines rebellion in terms of a struggle against inequality passing itself off as equality.[25] Rebellion in his view is always an affirmation of all humanity. "I rebel; therefore we exist."[26] To live the life of a brave sinner is to live as a Cross-bound rebel, rebelling against all the chaos, meaninglessness, evil, and injustice that mark human life in the names of Christ and love.

Brave Sinners Have Fun

With all the confidence that brave sinners can have, with their perspective that life is play as children enjoy, it is hardly surprising that brave sinners would find a lot of fun in life. I've already noted above one text written by Luther in which he refers to the happiness that accompanies an awareness of God's grace.[27] The Reformer has a lot to say about the joy that accompanies a Christian life marked by brave sinning. He is recorded as saying over table late in 1531:

> God wants us to be cheerful and He hates sadness. For had He wanted us to be sad, He would not have given us the sun, the moon and the various fruits of the earth. All these He gave for our good cheer.[28]

Note how the Reformer points to contemplation of realities beyond the self (the sun, the moon, and the fruits of the earth) as a means to happiness. Elsewhere, while expositing Psalm 126 he again associates this transcendent faith with joy by suggesting that we have as much laughter as we have faith.[29] Lecturing on Isaiah in 1532 he also asserted: "We can mark our lack of faith by our joy; for our joy must necessarily be as great as our faith."[30]

We need to emphasize at this point that for Luther this joy is not based on ourselves or our situation in life. It is based solely on the hope that Christ's work provides.[31] In other words, Luther's advice (and it is medically sound, as we shall see) is that you will not find happiness by seeking it through changing yourself or your circumstances. Happiness comes as a happy and unexpected gift of God though faith.[32]

The happiness associated with spirituality permeates all dimensions of life in Luther's view. Just getting away from yourself by getting in the company of others was sometimes enough to make you happy (along with a few beers and a little female companionship).

> Having been taught by experience, I can say how you ought to restore your spirit when you suffer from spiritual depression. When you are assailed by gloom, despair, or a troubled conscience you should eat, drink, and talk with others. If you can find help yourself by thinking of a girl, do so.[33]

Luther expresses this appreciation of the joy you can have with a good drink and some fellowship with direct reference to our relationship with Christ. Referring to the idea that in Justification the faithful are united to Christ in an intimate union, he spoke of this relationship with special intensity in his famed 1520 treatise, *The Freedom of a Christian*. The faithful, he claimed, having emptied themselves with a bold confession of their sin, are so totally saturated by God as to be inebriated, or intoxicated with Christ. He wrote:

> Since these promises of God are holy, true, righteous, free, and peaceful words, full of goodness, the soul which clings to them with a firm faith will be so closely united with them and altogether absorbed by them that it not only will

share in all their power but will be saturated and intoxicated by them.[34]

Brave sinners, it seems, are drunk on God. That is why good works come so spontaneously for Christians. They are so out of their mind with God in Christ, they just can't help themselves in doing God's thing. But just like somebody who's getting drunk at the party may have some fun getting there, so Christian life is a joyous inebriated party for the brave sinner. You don't need to be so uptight about all your important responsibilities, about what you need to please God. Brave sinners know that those activities aren't so important after all. In fact, showing love, seeking justice for the poor, making peace, comforting those in despair are just games to play. That takes the pressure off. Brave sinners don't take themselves so seriously. But they are so drunk on God that he'll make sure that those activities accomplish his aims, do some good through us. It is like the Reformer said in a sermon in the late 1530s on John that I'll quote subsequently. In it he claimed that Christians cannot help but bear fruit in all they do, that as a result everything comes easy and without burden to them.[35]

This image of being intoxicated with Christ, like the image of life as play, are two more testimonies to Luther's God-centered vision of the Christian life as a joyful, fun way to live. But Luther believed that along with joy there is one other benefit that accrues to the life of a brave sinner. In a 1532 comment over dinner he boldly contended:

I should be so joyful that I ought to be entirely well for joy; and for very joy it ought to be impossible for me to become sick.[36]

Brave sinning (and we'll see why in the next chapter) is good for your health.

I've already suggested why a life that deems its various relationships and events as play should bring joy. The life of brave sinning, with its courageous confession of sin and recognition of our inability to do any good without God, renders us God-centered at the core of our being. This God-centeredness in the life of brave sinners is also a factor in giving them a life of joy, as they likely have a lot more fun in their rebelliousness than those who are purpose driven, chasing prosperity, or just living narcissistically. Showered with God's grace, confident in and focused on God's love for us, brave sinners have the courage to challenge and concupiscently to yearn for an end to the meaningless status quo in which we live, but to have fun doing it.

The Bible testifies to the joy of a life spirituality centered on God (or at least centered on projects bigger than the self). The joy of such spirituality is expressed in the book of Psalms (1:1–2): "Happy are those who do not follow the advice of the wicked . . . but their delight is in the Law of the Lord, and on His Law they meditate day and night." And again in Psalms 128:1 we read, "Happy is everyone who fears the Lord . . ."; and in 144:15, ". . . happy are the people whose God is the Lord." As we'll see in the next chapter, there are good scientific reasons for such joy.

Brave Sinning Makes for a Joyful Life!

Neurobiological Data

I have now made the case for brave sinning as a lifestyle that promises a lot more fun than a purpose-driven life or a life striving for prosperity. The brave sinner is someone so totally dependent on God that he or she looks at life, even the most important projects, as play. They are play, because what we do has no ultimate significance unless God makes it significant. Cutting-edge Neurobiological research indicates that when human beings forget themselves in this way, and—like players in a game—become concentrated on aims and priorities bigger than they are as individuals, they activate parts of the brain that are in turn bathed in pleasurable chemicals providing sensations of happiness. And these chemicals, it seems, are also good for your health. Having a worldview like brave sinning that does not deny our concupiscent, rebellious yearnings and the joys of play, but gets the focus off ourselves in the quest for these pleasures, affords the sort of self-transcendence and God-centeredness that activates these salubrious neurochemical processes.[1] In that sense, Martin Luther is correct: Christians really are drunk on Christ, inebriated with the brain chemicals that produce joy.

A BRIEF INTRODUCTION TO THE HUMAN BRAIN

Genes are of course the informational building blocks of the human brain, making possible the 100 billion *neurons* (brain cells) which comprise this 3-pound lump of wrinkled tissue serving as the seat of the mind. The neurons themselves consist of cell bodies and a number of fibers clothed by and interconnected with grayish nerve tissue called *gray matter*. Neurons are the communication cells of the brain. These cells carry information and are capable of transmitting electrical currents which are the agents of this communication.

Unlike other cells of the human body, neurons include thread-like extensions of themselves or fibers of neurons called *dendrites* that carry these currents. Dendrites generate and transmit electrical currents to neurons when they receive electrical pulses from other neurons. The interconnections between neurons in the gray matter enable the brain to interpret signals from sense organs, compare them with memories, and plan suitable action.

Communication between entities is one thing. Physical interconnections like neurons (gray matter) make are something distinct from mere communication. Something new is created. This process also includes the general nerve fibers called *white matter*, which connect the brain's cortex (its outer portion) to the rest of the human nervous system, enhancing communication of the brain with the entire body. But within the brain itself, not all its neurons are interconnected. That is a blessing, for if they were, the possibility of forging new neural connections (and so enabling the transmission of new knowledge) would not be possible. On the contrary, new connections are always being formed in the healthy and active human brain. In that sense we can speak of the brain as being self-organized.[2] The brain is also assisted in building these neural connections by certain brain chemicals called *monoamines*, which when triggered by the electrical impulses caused by neural *dendrites* (branched projections of neuron fibers connecting with other neurons), ferry signals from one neuron to another that in turn facilitate the binding of these neurons. And when these chemicals are experienced as pleasurable the connections forged between neurons are reinforced and more likely to be retained. These insights about the brain have redirected research in neurology in exciting directions.

RECENT NEUROLOGICAL FINDINGS

Several research teams, most notably one led by Andrew Newberg, the Director of Nuclear Medicine at the University of Pennsylvania Hospital, have demonstrated that in moments of deepest spiritual experience and self-transcendence the human brain's *frontal lobe* and especially its *prefrontal cortex* (the frontal lobe's gray matter that connects various neurological cells) were subject to the most blood flow and therefore the most active. By contrast, the posterior *parietal lobe*, which functions as the neurological region orienting the self in time and space, defining the self's desires, went blank. Similar results have been identified by National Institutes of Health researcher Dean Hamer.[3] Spirituality, it seems, is not likely to be experienced when we are too preoccupied with our own present circumstances, personal satisfaction, or our own feelings. The observation has profound implications for evaluating the spirituality nurtured by Prosperity Gospel preaching or a theology that overemphasizes *my* purpose.

The frontal lobe's gray matter, the frontal cortex (especially the prefrontal cortex), is also the part of the brain responsible for thinking and planning. Consequently, similar dynamics seem to transpire whenever we focus on a project bigger than our own present circumstances, personal satisfaction, or feelings.[4]

Other dynamics are involved in spiritual experience as well as in the brain's thinking and planning functions. It seems that when the left frontal lobe is activated there is also increased activity deep inside the brain in its *limbic system*—the part of the brain which is the seat of emotions.[5]

Emotions, good feelings, are a function of monoamines.[6] One type of monoamine, *serotonin*, combats depression. But another such chemical, *dopamine*, is the "feel-good" natural drug, comprised of hydrogen, oxygen, carbon, and nitrogen, but with properties related to amphetamines and cocaine. Some cells in the *basal ganglia* (knots of interconnected nerve cells located deep within the brain) produce this pleasurable monoamine and send it to the forebrain and its prefrontal cortex.[7]

Both Newberg and Hamer have identified higher levels of dopamine in spiritual experiences, or at least among those who regularly practice spirituality. Hamer has proceeded to identify the gene VMAT2 as the key agent in integrating primary and higher consciousness in the human brain. Its purpose is to control the flow of monoamines in the brain. It seems that this gene had some variants, and these variants have implications for self-transcendence. Individuals analyzed who had the VMAT2 gene which contained the nucleic acid *cystonine* in one particular spot ranked higher on self-transcendence than those with the nucleic acid *adenine* in the same spot.[8]

Apparently what transpires is that when VMAT2 does not vigorously function in transmitting monoamines like dopamine to brain vessels, the dopamine is degraded by cellular enzymes. In order for the dopamine to flow into the prefrontal cortex it needs to be released by the cells, and before that, such monoamines must be wrapped up by membranes. VMAT2 is the gene that weaves in and out of the tiny spheres of the membranes, enclosing the dopamine and other monoamines. It forms a channel across the membrane, acting as the border crossing for dopamine and other monoamines. When such monoamines are wrapped with membranes they remain shielded until they are stimulated by pulses of electronic energy from other cells. When that happens the VMAT2 transporter is like a channel across the membrane, a kind of border crossing for the brain chemical. Research by Hamer and George Uhl suggests that if we do not have the right kind of VMAT2 the dopamine does not flow as freely into the cells of the frontal lobe (will not be experienced as a significant alteration of the monoamine signaling). By contrast, people with more dopamine flowing in spiritual experiences are more likely to find these activities urgent and in turn experience a more profound sense of joy and fulfillment. Amidst much fanfare, this has led Hamer to refer to VMAT2 as the "God gene."[9]

Things may not be quite this simple. The scientific community has raised numerous critiques of Hamer's claim to have identified the "God gene." Among those challenging his conclusion on grounds of the minimal evidence he has produced are science writer Carl Zimmer and Neurobiologist Mario Beauregard.[10] Likewise, even Newberg's findings regarding the prefrontal cortex as the seat of spirituality have been challenged at least to some extent by Beauregard on methodological grounds. He has also conducted subsequent brain-imaging studies of Carmelite nuns caught up in mystical experiences, employing a different analytic technique, *functional magnetic resonance* (imaging the production of brain change images by means of radio waves in a strong magnetic field), rather than *positron emission tomography* (imaging brain activity using emissions from decaying radioactive isotopes [forms of brain elements with chemical properties closely related to those parts of the brain studied]) employed by Newberg. Beauregard and his colleagues found that several brain regions were activated in these experiences. Cerebral blood flow in the subjects seems to have increased not just in the prefrontal cortex (as Newberg and his colleagues found), but also in their *inferior frontal lobe*, the *inferior parietal lobe*, the *superior parietal lobe*, and their *temporal cortices*.[11]

Although this new data might seem to contradict Newberg's findings, neither Beauregard nor Newberg himself thinks that to be the case. Thus, Beauregard notes that the activation of the parietal cortex might simply be a function of the parietal region during mystical experience, not a driving force in the experience; instead it merely reflects a modification of the body schema associated with the impression that something greater than the individual is about to absorb him or her. And Newberg takes into account other studies of those engaged in spiritual experiences that point to the activation of neurological regions not clearly identified as busy centers of blood flow in his studies. He explains the activation of the brain's *thalamus* (gray matter at the posterior region of the forebrain) in spiritual experiences. Insofar as the thalamus provides the superior parietal lobe with sensory information, it follows that Newberg's recognition of the increased blood flow in the prefrontal cortex during spiritual exercises still allows for some impact on the parietal lobe and would likewise activate the thalamus (at least insofar as in such self-transcendent experiences the prefrontal cortex stimulates a diminution of sensory input which in turn has implications for alterations in the thalamus' activity).[12]

It is apparent that the data which seem to challenge the findings of Newberg and Hamer do not ultimately discredit their basic insights. When experiencing the transcendent (in spiritual experiences), the prefrontal lobe and its cortex, bathed in dopamine, go into overdrive while the parietal lobe goes dim (or at least does not set the agenda for the brain). Religious people characteristically lose themselves in the transcendent—and it feels good. There is a paradoxical relationship involved in experiencing transcendence: while becoming less preoccupied with oneself, our selfish quest for pleasure is actually requited (at least for awhile). As we'll see, we also are likely to adopt a lifestyle that will keep us healthier and give us more happiness, prompted by the increased levels of dopamine in the brain. The religious life is not so devoid of self-ishness after all. It is not unmarred by sin, but is an activity that is, as Martin Luther contended, simultaneously both righteous and sinful. Neurobiological data next to be considered support the vision of Christian life as brave sinning. Being religious (cen-tered on the transcendent) and self-forgetful is pleasurable (and so marred by selfishness).

Happiness and Health: New Neuroscientific Insights

There have been some interesting discoveries in contemporary Neuropsychology about what physically makes us happy and how these elements relate to health. Intriguingly, these bodily dynamics parallel the neural processes of spirituality I have been discussing.

I have already noted the role of monoamines in the brain, how they relay messages from one nerve cell in the brain to others, pro-viding pleasurable sensations that reinforce these connections. The brain is always seeking to create new nerve connections. This pro-cess is especially stimulated by gaining new knowledge or enjoying new experiences. Monoamines facilitate the pleasurable sensations associated with these examples.[13]

It is helpful to be reminded here of the role dopamine plays in spiritual experiences. Functioning to provide a kind of drug-like high, dopamine is the neurotransmitter most involved in the experience of happiness, bliss, or desire. It has several pleasurable results: It heightens awareness of interesting situations, waking us up to life's amusements. It also stimulates pleasurable experiences for the brain's dendrites (which enable the process for the whole body to enjoy pleasure); in fact, dopamine causes the dendrites to remember good experiences. In addition, dopamine serves to con-trol our muscles, to ensure that when the brain gives orders, the rest of the body executes what we have willed. Not surprisingly, as mentioned earlier, dopamine creates a "high" that motivates and activates a response. Under the influence of dopamine the brain learns to make new connections, creating a pleasure cycle wherein nerve impulses are passed from one cell to another, more connections are established in the brain, and more cells release dopamine and its pleasurable reactions.

Monoamines like dopamine are not freely available to the brain. They are produced in the brain cells (neurons). In the case of dopamine, it is produced as we have noted by cells in the midbrain's basal ganglia identified with motor control, the *ventral tegmental*. The chemical is also believed to be produced by neighboring nerve cells termed the *substantia nigra*. These neuron clusters send these neurotransmitters either to the *striatum*, which facilitates and regulates bodily motion or, most relevant for our interests, to the executive portion of the brain, the prefrontal cortex.

Through his work at the University of Wisconsin-Madison, Neuropsychologist Richard Davidson has confirmed that dopamine makes people feel good. Of course this is hardly surprising given its cocaine-like chemical composition. Davidson and his colleagues have proceeded to establish a link between prefrontal-lobe activity and bliss. There seems to be a similar link in this part of the brain between spiritual experience and happiness. Significantly, Davidson came to his conclusions by attaching electrodes to various Buddhist monks' skulls while they meditated. It became clear that in their moments of reported bliss, the prefrontal cortex (especially on the left side of the frontal lobe, charged with operating proactively to enhance our well-being) was most active.

As the seat of executive functions for the brain and the receptor of dopamine, that the prefrontal cortex would be more active than other segments when we are happy makes sense. The left prefrontal lobe's purpose in regulating the brain's neural connections entails that the pleasurable sensations resulting from the flow of dopamine to these particular brain cells has implications for the whole brain. And if the brain in its entirety is governed by such pleasure, it stands to reason that the whole person experiences happiness. Ultimately, then, Davidson and his colleagues have identified as a proximate cause of happiness an active left prefrontal area of the brain, which is an especially sensitive receptor of the dopamine and soaks it up in quantity.[14] When you are planning or thinking about something bigger than you are (such as in encounters with a loving God), you are likely to be happier, because the part of your brain that impacts all neurological cells will be more likely bathed with dopamine. (Likewise, when you are thankfully remembering, a process also facilitated by dopamine, the happier you are likely to be.[15] At least Christian faith and worship are about such remembering, viewing life in the context of remembered stories.) This insight that we find joy in working on things that are bigger than we are, even though ultimately these activities are finite and will pass away, is expressed powerfully in Ecclesiastes. The same author who could lament "I hate all my toil in which I had toiled under the sun, seeing that I must leave it to those who come after me" (2:18), and "What do mortals get from all the toil and strain with which they toil under the Sun? For all their days are full of pain, and their work is a vexation; even at night their minds do not rest" (2:23), could proclaim: "There is nothing better for mortals than to eat and drink and find enjoyment in their toil . . ." (2:24; 3:13). Similarly Proverbs 14:21 proclaims the joy that comes from helping others: ". . . but happy are those who are kind to the poor."

I've already discussed the various biblical texts indicating that a God-centered life leads to happiness. Poll data can be cited to certify the conclusion that experiencing transcendence—that faith—makes you happy. Most obvious is the finding of the Gallup Poll in late 2007 that regular churchgoers have a higher level of happiness than the American public as a whole by nearly 10 percent.[16]

There is a growing pool of neurological data that supports the conclusion that being religious, especially the happiness that goes with it, is good for your health. Richard Davidson's research indicates that happy people with active left prefrontal cortexes have lower levels of *cortisol*, a hormone that depresses immune function and causes unseemly body configuration.[17] When we spiritually engage in projects larger than ourselves, it seems that there are more of our natural resources available for fighting disease.

The dopamine associated with both happiness and religious experience also has salubrious consequences for promoting health. It stimulates social behavior. Those saturated with it, like religious people are, have been found less likely to engage in antisocial behavior or to be addicted to drugs.[18]

Psychologists Laura Kubzansky and Laura Richman found that hopefulness and curiosity seem protective against hypertension, diabetes, and upper-respiratory infection. Kubzansky also found that heart disease rates among men who called themselves optimistic were half the rates of men who didn't. Dopamine makes a significant contribution to this hopefulness, which springs from this monoamine's role in alleviating pain.[19]

Psychologist Robert Emmons likewise conducted studies of 1,000 adults showing that those who kept gratitude journals were not only happier, but practiced better health promotion. Emmons and his colleagues also concede that such gratitude is very much the province of religion.[20] The new scientific data is unambiguous. Religion (especially when it is centered on a transcendent perspective pushing you away from a preoccupation with your own present circumstances) not only makes you happy, but it is also good for your health.

In view of these neurological dynamics, it makes sense to contend that Martin Luther's vision of religion and the Christian life in particular is likely to enhance that dopamine flow as well as its salubrious effects even more markedly than alternative spiritualities. Brave sinners are not simply self-forgetful, focused on transcendent realities. Recall that the Reformers often spoke of the sinner's relationship to Christ like that of a bride and groom. And inasmuch as loving couples enjoy increased dopamine flow (love feels good), thinking of Jesus in terms of such a love relationship seems also likely to trigger yet more dopamine along with the happiness and health it brings.[21]

Qualifications

There are a number of issues that need to be resolved before I'll be entirely comfortable with all the connections I have sketched between Luther's concept of brave sinning and the latest Neurobiological findings. But even if ultimately the relationships noted are superficial, the life of brave sinning and its freedom from the Law and guilt has Warren's duty-bound purpose-driven style of life and the quest for prosperity beat as far as which one is the most joyful way to live. So I'll keep standing with Luther's model even if the connections with Neurobiology break down.

For example, it might be argued that the points I've raised effectively diminish the uniqueness of Christian spirituality. Most of the Neurobiological research on spirituality has focused on the brain activity of Buddhist monks in meditation. One might contend, then, that in applying scientific observation about the brain patterns of these monks to Christian spirituality I have effectively identified Christian faith with Buddhism. (I will concede that in my own life journey I have discerned some profound compatibilities between the Buddhist model of liberation from karma, from the chains of human existence, and the Christian vision of liberation from our sinful condition.) Both are about a self-emptying existence free from the bondage of ego addiction. Given these conceptual compatibilities should we be surprised that each would give rise to similar neurological operations? But that is not to say that the truth-claims of each religion are identical. It is much different to live actively and joyfully in the world, enveloped in the arms of a loving and affirming God than it is to pass away into the oblivion of nothingness as Buddhists believe.

Another apparently problematic implication of relating Christian spirituality to Neurobiological insights about spiritual experience is evident in the saturation with dopamine that the spiritual man or woman experiences. Dopamine, recall, is a chemical whose effect, like any drug, wears off. Eventually spirituality and the happiness it engenders would not continue to be satisfying.

The Bible also seems to intuit what modern science tells us about happiness wearing off—about the tolerance we build up to dopamine. Proverbs 14:13 reads: "Even in laughter the heart is sad, and the end of joy is grief." What, then, explains the perdurance of spirituality? I have been wondering if *oxytocin* might be the answer.

Oxytocin is an amino acid peptide produced by a structure deep in the brain connected to the pituitary gland called the *hypothalamus*. Its primary task is to manage the automatic nervous system and behaviors related to survival, including sex. Especially when mothers are nursing or when long-term heterosexual couples are intimate, the hypothalamus produces significant levels of oxytocin. Once produced, this acid is sent to the pituitary gland, which in turn secretes it to different sections of the brain, especially to a group of cells higher and more in the front of the brain, the *nucleus accumbens*.

Oxytocin seems to trigger the creation of deep feelings, which in turn provide a foundation for love and trust. It is also good for the health—lowering blood pressure, stimulating cell division (a mark of youth), and healing wounds. This neurochemical may also enhance long-term attachments insofar as it eventually sends signals to the brain's *caudate nuclei*, a pair of structures on either side of the head. These segments of the brain store data concerning mundane habits like walking and snapping fingers that are never forgotten. Other behaviors like love that oxytocin stores in this part of the brain entail that they more than likely will not be forgotten. Could it be that oxytocin might play a role in spirituality, in which case we might be able to explain the perdurance of faith?

After all, the higher the oxytocin dose the more salubrious impact it has on your body and life. And unlike dopamine, it does not appear that you can ever develop an immunity to it.[22]

To date there is no hard evidence that oxytocin saturates the brain in spiritual exercises. But insofar as oxytocin is secreted in long-term love relationships as the effectiveness of dopamine wears off, and also when we recall Luther's notion of justification by grace as a kind of marital union with Christ, it seems reasonable to speculate the possibility that, as we continue living with Jesus in a spiritually loving relationship as Luther construes it, the faithful might start to experience oxytocin. This possibility seems certainly worth further research.

CONCLUSION: A MORE JOYFUL SPIRITUALLY CENTERED LIFE

I have now made the scientific case for the conclusion that people receive both happiness and health from spirituality. In that sense spirituality and self-transcendence are marred by selfishness, and so sin. These activities are the bravest of sins.

Brave sinners get pleasurable results from faith no less than Warren and Osteen claim that there are benefits for the self in living with purpose or seeking prosperity. The difference is that brave sinners know they are sinning in a self-seeking way that Warren and Osteen never acknowledge. While for these two men, then, the self-seeking is natural, good, and righteous, brave sinners know that their self-seeking is sin. This entails that they have a built-in critical perspective on it, are less likely to reduce all that there is to a narcissist expression of their own self-seeking.

The awareness of sin also gets you out of your narcissist box, as in order for brave sinners to do any good they need God, not just as a vehicle of self-seeking. A courageous affirmation of your sin makes you more dependent on God and so breaks the self-seeking cycle of Narcissism. But if your self-seeking is construed as good and righteous, you just continue on in your selfishness. Your parietal lobe, orienting your activities to your spatial and temporal circumstances, is still active. You get some of the dopamine pleasures when you are focused, seeking purpose or prosperity (for all concentrated activity of the prefrontal cortex is rewarded with some dopamine). But your focus in these exercises is still on yourself and your context, not on how your actions affect a greater good. More so than in Warren's purpose-driven vision, the life of brave sinning makes the joy of devotion more unambiguously God-centered, and so that life is more likely to saturate the brain with higher doses of dopamine—more unambiguous delight.

The God-centered perspective of brave sinning, its abandon of our own space-time circumstances (in the sense of undermining their importance by reducing all our actions to mere joyful play), renders brave sinners countercultural rebels. And this means that brave sinners are better positioned to change America than Rick Warren and Prosperity Gospel preachers are.

How Brave Sinning
Could Change
American Life

In trying to outline how a church committed to propagating and enjoying a life of brave sinning could change American life, let's start by reviewing what's happening today in America and in Western culture in general. I have already provided ample evidence of the impact of Narcissism on American and Western European society. Consequently I'll focus first in this chapter on the economic trends. It's not a happy picture, even for brave sinners who have fun with their spirituality (unless you're rich). Of course, front-brain-oriented brave sinners, not so hung up on themselves, will not mind getting their hands dirty in the garbage (are not above all the egocentricity involved in political engagement) and are less likely to be attracted by all the garbage we'll consider. Brave sinners are more likely to be the rebellious, other-centered activists you can trust, because at least they'll be brave in confessing their temptations as well as their abuse of the power and influence they have. They are also, in the spirit of Camus, ready to rebel against the inequality passing itself off as equality in our feel-good ethos.

THE RAT RACE AND ITS LOSERS

Americans may have become ensconced in excessive individualism, in a Narcissism that only concerns them about their own welfare, but they clearly do not know how to have fun, at least not as much as their European counterparts. A 2007 report of the International Labour Organization showed that Americans work more hours than workers in any other industrialized nation. Various studies provide us with the hard data of this rat race. A recent report of the U.S. Census Bureau notes that 28 percent of the American labor force works more than 40 hours per week. Eight percent work more than 60 hours. A study of the National Sleep Foundation indicates that the average employed American works 47.5 hours per week. An earlier report had indicated that 38 percent of Americans work more than 50 hours each week.[1]

Things are no better with regard to taking vacation breaks. Expedia Survey reported on April 15, 2008, that the average annual vacation granted by American businesses to full-time workers is just fourteen days. But more than one-third of American workers do not use the allotted time.[2]

Oh, but Americans are happy working this hard and advancing their careers, some might contend. The polls report that Americans have high degrees of satisfaction. Indeed an early 2008 Gallup Poll reported, before the impact of the recession had been felt, that 8 in 10 Americans say they are happy (52 percent "very happy," 40 percent "fairly happy," 6 percent "not too happy"). But this is down from 55 percent of the population who said they were "very happy" in 2004.

Consider what these statistics imply. Half of the population in pre-recession America was not very happy. And a slightly older Gallup Poll indicated that a little less than half of the middle class (those earning $30,000 to $74,000) falls in this category. When you get to the working class, two-thirds of that demographic is not happy and also two-thirds of those not married are not fully enjoying life. You've got to be rich (earning $75,000 or more per year) in order to find a category in which nearly two-thirds of the American public is very happy.[3] It just shows that money doesn't really buy you happiness.

One other matter needs to be considered in this connection. It is commonly noted in polling circles that those surveyed are not always honest in answering questions about religion, sex, or happiness. Cowardly sinners are prone to report deeper spirituality and more satisfaction than they actually experience or feel. We have already considered some data that calls into question whether the number of Americans who say they are really happy is in fact an accurate and truthful count. If 18 percent of American women and 13 percent of men (not to mention 23 percent of the Baby Boomers) have been to a therapist, it seems hard to believe that as many people who report satisfaction really are as happy as they claim to be.[4]

The other data challenging the Gallup Poll's findings about the happiness of Americans is evident in a 2006 National Household Survey on Drug Use and Health. As of 2005, this most recent national survey found 112 million Americans older than age 11 reported having used illicit drugs (45 percent of the population). In fact, 15 percent of Americans had reportedly used such drugs in the past year.[5]

Recall the discussion in chapter 5 of the neurobiological dimensions of a life lived sinning bravely. I noted at this time that happiness is experienced when the brain is bathed in monoamines (brain chemicals that ferry signals from one brain neuron to others). Two of these important monoamines are dopamine (a precursor to adrenaline, similar in structure to amphetamines) and serotonin (a brain chemical with similar structure), the latter of which functions to thwart negative emotions, while the former provides the brain with motivation and pleasurable rewards for exercising the frontal lobe with its executive and self-forgetful functions. Happy people experience the free and regular flow of these natural drugs. No need for such people artificially to re-create these natural highs. Consequently, we can only conclude that the illicit drug users are not themselves happy. Do the math—it follows that at best we are lucky if half the American public is really happy. I've already suggested that this dismal statistic is a matter of not having enough brave sinners in American society. I'll return again to that point later in the chapter.

The American rat race is not ultimately satisfying, even for the winners. Let's talk about the losers, and the likelihood of you and your children joining that number.

Poverty and the Uninsured

The scandal of contemporary American society is that the richest nation in the world, if not in history, allows its people to live in squalor. An August 26, 2008, report of the U.S. Census Bureau reports that 37.3 million Americans (12.5 percent of the population) were in poverty in 2007. It is staggering to keep in mind that more than one in ten Americans suffer poverty.

Such poverty risks health, not just for oneself, but also for entire families. Poor people, indeed the working class, cannot afford health insurance, especially not with the growing costs of such insurance. The National Center for Health Statistics reports that 18.2 percent of the American population (nearly 54 million people) were without health insurance in 2007.[6]

This situation is especially dire in America. The Organization for Economic Cooperation and Development in 2008 reported that America has the widest gap between the rich and poor of any high-income nation in the world. Over 30 percent of American income is in the hands of the richest 10 percent of the population; only 1.8 percent of income is in the hands of the poorest 10 percent.[7]

It is a very unhappy picture (if you are self-transcendent after the fashion of brave sinners). For a brave sinner aiming to forget himself or herself to serve the neighbor will sense disappointment when the neighbor's lot is not good. On the other hand, Narcissists, caught up in the mad chase for self-fulfillment, are less likely to be concerned. A 2000 Harris poll indicates that 75 percent of all adult Americans believe that most people on welfare would find work if they were not on welfare. A plurality (45 percent) believe that most people who are poor should blame themselves for their poverty.[8]

In fact, though, Narcissistic Americans should be concerned. Unless they are among the wealthiest Americans, there is some significant chance that their children or grandchildren could be candidates for poverty. An April 2006 report by the Center for American Progress provides some disturbing information. It seems that there is a much higher social mobility in France, Germany, Sweden, Canada, Finland, Norway, and Denmark than in the United States. Children of low-income families have only a 1 percent chance of reaching the top 5 percent of income distribution. By contrast the children of the rich have a 22 percent chance of reaching this income level.

Being born into a middle-class home is no longer the springboard to a better life. Children born to the middle fifth of parental family income ($42,000 to $54,300) have the same chance of ending up in a lower income level as moving to a higher level. They only have a 1.8 percent chance of attaining the top 5 percent of income levels. Another disturbing fact: There is still a significant difference in mobility for Blacks and whites.[9]

NO WAY OUT FOR THE NARCISSIST AND THE PURPOSE-DRIVEN

A society largely populated by Narcissists, by people dedicated to their own immediate gratification even to the point of regarding the "other" as a mere tool for enhancing self-interest, with a media committed to nurturing such a lifestyle, will have no

time and little sympathy for anyone but themselves, certainly
not to help the poor through commitment to social change.
Such a society will not do much to get us out of the rat race
either. Caught up in the emptiness of the self, addicted to the
acclaim that comes from being important or accumulating an
audience through their perceived indispensability, and at least in
some cases hoping that the accumulation of wealth can provide
this, Narcissists will continue to work the long hours without
respite, and without starting a movement to challenge such an
economically mandated lifestyle. Besides, caught up as they are
in themselves, and so, as noted in the previous chapter, prone to
activate the rear parts of their brain (the parietal lobe), Narcissists
and a society populated with such people will not experience the
happiness that the brain enjoys when its natural dope (the monoamines) flows as a result of the activation of the self-denying,
front parts of the brain (especially the left prefrontal cortex). This
sort of society is not comprised of enough people with the sufficient self-confidence that comes with being happy enough with
oneself to enact change.

Given our present sociological and psychological dynamics,
don't expect things to change without a significant social endorsement of the worldview of brave sinning. Generally speaking, the
most influential spiritual/religious options of our day will not
provide it. In a recent book I described in detail why the prevailing theological models of Western academic institutions (both
Protestant and Catholic) as well as those of the Right (including
the supporters of the so-called Prosperity Gospel) can't do the
job. The academy is so ensconced in the intellectual suppositions
which have nurtured Narcissism and the options of the Right have
so embedded themselves in the religious convictions of the Puritan
Paradigm that these theological options do not have the critical
distance on the developments we have been describing to make a
genuine critique possible.[10] They do not nurture the sort of rebellious perspective on life that brave sinning does.

We have been observing how this critique must be applied to Rick Warren. His purpose-driven vision also ultimately falls prey to Narcissist dispositions, and so will not be effective in positively influencing America regarding its responsibilities in the political spheres of social and economic justice. He would have us favor our Christian friends (those sharing our interests) over the mass of humanity. Even his vision of community, as I mentioned, is more a refuge from the world than an agent for social change.[11]

This privatizing of religion logically connects with Warren's conception of and concentration on the purpose of individuals. Even when he does speak of the purpose-driven church or engages in his ministry to fight AIDS in Africa he is not addressing the social and political dynamics necessary to endure the rat race. No less than the Narcissist, we should not expect Rick Warren's vision of Christianity to change America. Nor, for all its virtues, will his theological position ultimately succeed to help us stop being the kind of people we have become.

WHAT KIND OF PEOPLE HAVE WE BECOME? THE DIFFERENCE GRACE AND BRAVE SINNING CAN MAKE IN OUR LIVES AND IN OUR NATION

In a way we have been answering this question. A combination of the therapeutic ethos, the media, the economy, and our own selfish, concupiscent dispositions have turned us into self-addicted, individualistic Narcissists. As such, we are a lot lonelier and insecure than we admit. We also don't stand for much, since the things we live for are just passing fads.

The flexible economy formed in the era of the computer revolution has shaped another form of Narcissism, contributing to the emergence of a distinct, but related personality type. Today's business world has perpetuated an ethos in which there is an indifference to one's fellows, since they are disposable to the flexible corporation.[12] One result of these dynamics is that a new kind of personality has come to be accepted within the American economy. Rather than the older model of driven man, so characteristic of the Industrial Age, the new economy's demand for teamwork and flexibility have nurtured ironic personalities—people who can never take too seriously what they say or do, because they must always be open or subject to change.[13]

The ironic character type is Narcissistic. Such people are willing to compromise what they stand for in order to advance their careers. They stand for nothing; they are empty. And not just in business do we find this character type today: Political leaders, leaders in public education as well as in higher education, even church leaders need to learn to stand aloof from what they have just said (to "learn from their mistakes" is the politically correct parlance to be used to justify such value flexibility) in order to keep everyone happy and maintain their power. Of course if my life is all about gaining acclaim, if the things I do and stand for, even with regard to the people to whom I seem to be accountable, are just tools to have me gain the acclaim I want, then not only am I alone, but I am also empty (like the Narcissist), and fundamentally unhappy.

Rick Warren's idea of purpose has a real point in ministering to this sort of Narcissism. It could provide the ironic personality with something for which to stand. But, as we have observed, as long as the focus is still on what the individual must do to live out that purpose rather than on how God (or some great cause) is using us, the focus will be too much on the individual truly to break with the current isolated Narcissist ethos. An empty, insecure individual trying to discern or execute her or his purpose will not find joy—that person may be too centered on the back part of the brain to think about what can be done for others, or even to be rebelliously confident enough permanently to stand for something.

Only the grace of God, an awareness of the unconditional love of God, is able to turn around the ironic personality. Martin Luther and his concept of being united with Christ in a kind of marital union provides insight as to how God's love changes lives, fills the emptiness that narcissist society has foisted on us. Luther wrote: "Our empty Law is ended by Christ Who fills the vacuum. . . ."[14]

We have been noticing in the previous chapters how the concept of brave sinning helps to solidify this sort of total dependence on God. Let's review why this is the case. When you totally renounce your goodness as brave sinners do, then such people must depend without equivocation on God for all the good in their lives. The vacuum of goodness in their lives can then be filled by good in Christ. This dependence on God has all sort of salubrious consequences.

Recall that people totally dependent on God (and brave sinners always aware of their sin have nowhere else to go than to God's grace) are so inclined to renounce themselves that the executive, transcendent aspects of the brain (especially the frontal lobe) goes into overdrive, just as the parietal lobe which is active when we are concerned about our personal circumstances becomes inactive. When it is activated, this executive part of the brain, especially the left prefrontal cortex of the lobe (the outer layer of gray matter of the lobe), is bathed in pleasurable neurochemicals, especially dopamine.[15] The brain's mechanisms, noted earlier, clearly aim to reinforce this sort of transcendent, even spiritual activity. Spirituality on this side of the Fall into sin feels good. As such, faith is not really selfless, but is itself mired in sin—is in fact a brave sin!

Depending on God (spirituality) makes you happy. Geneticists have observed that this sort of experience, especially coupled with the believer's tendency to forget oneself (with the dimming of activity in the parietal lobe in the back of the brain), leads to an optimism to press on regardless of the hardships faced.[16] The combination of feeling good and affirmed as well as living a life not dreading mortality—because one has lived dying to the things of this world—gives confidence for facing death. That leads to courage, to a willingness to risk, even when the going gets tough. The brave sinner, dependent on grace, is no longer ironic, but is ready to live with an unchanging fidelity to the Giver of these gifts and his values—the Ten Commandments.

The grace of God and brave sinning can make a difference to America and to the world—nurturing people who are no longer ironic, empty, and narcissistically self-concerned. With more faithful brave sinners, society becomes more other-directed and a little happier. We would likely find more time for our children, rather than investing it in our latest gadget or pursuit of self-fulfillment. We clearly would not be a society that needed as much therapy or drugs as we do. Who needs therapy and drugs when the dopamine is flowing in the brain? But addressing our addictions, nurturing happier, more spiritually oriented people will not in itself change our society enough and make us a more just nation. There will never be enough brave sinners to make that possible. And besides, people who depend on God's grace in this way are still sinners and will always want things to happen to their advantage in society and government. It takes good laws and a just social order to keep these sinners and everybody else in line, to restrain our selfish impulses. That's why it's important to inject the characteristics of a faithful walk with Jesus and brave sinning into the political sphere if a fresh awareness of the love of God is really to change American life and Western society.

Politics Matter for Brave Sinners— But They Need Coalition Partners

Politics matter because brave sinners are still sinners. Brave sinners call our attention to the fact that we can never forget that even those totally dependent on grace are as selfish and concupiscent as they ever were.

I have previously noted the selfish character of genes. They will always do what is in their interests or whatever facilitates their propagation.[17] Also recall that the experience of transcendence and being bathed in the pleasurable neurochemicals that accompany it make you feel good. Even your faith is mixed with selfishness and concupiscence.

I have already observed that sinners (even the brave ones) need restraint. There will always need to be laws and social conventions in order to trim our selfish desires. Shorthanded as they are, politics also give brave sinners the opportunity to find coalition partners needed truly to change things in society.

Such a strategy makes common scientific sense, not just biblical sense. Just as it is not only Christians who have moral standards, since the Bible teaches that all human beings share a moral sense (Romans 2:14–15), so it isn't just brave sinners who can display the kind of confidence and joy (natural brain chemical highs) that come from caring for something bigger than you are. This experience is natural. It happens to anyone exercising the left prefrontal lobe of the brain.

Politically, all that Christian commitments provide the brave sinner with is a reinforcement to keep the front part of the brain active, more realism about human nature, and a little more affirmation of who they are. Brave sinners are not necessarily politically wiser than their (cowardly sinning) secularist counterparts. If we want to change America, brave-sinning Christians, aware of their shortcomings in certain technical areas, need to lean on the political insights of wiser non-Christians sometimes. Broad coalitions can be built between Christians and like-minded non-Christians in such ways as to exert significant political influence.

Not surprisingly, this perspective on Christian engagement in politics has long-time precedents in the theologies of St. Augustine (his idea of the two cities) and Martin Luther (and his concept of the Two-Kingdom Ethic). Both Augustine and Luther envisaged two modes of existence in the world, either living a life dedicated to the self or to God. Government's role, unlike that of the Church, is to restrain us when we are living life dedicated to self. But the proper means of restraint in this realm is not in their view the Gospel teachings of God's love, but the Law of God known by all human beings (the natural law). This is why their perspective on politics converges with my call for Christians to learn from the insights of non-Christians who have access to the natural law as much as Christians do. This convergence between my own political viewpoint and those of Augustine as well as his Reformation protege is to be expected given that the radical awareness of sin I have been stressing is rooted in their traditions. In any case the recognition of the brave sinner, that Christians have no special insights into politics, that Christians and non-Christians can collaborate in transforming society, was affirmed by both.[18] This viewpoint breaks with the American Puritan paradigm, which posits that Christian principles should govern society. Brave sinning and the vision of politics this worldview supports are countercultural. But it will take a countercultural Christianity to change American life.

Other implications for engaging the public sphere follow from understanding ourselves as brave sinners. Augustine summarizes one of them well. Government needs to restrain, not just concern itself with (Christian) values, because there is always a kind of civil war going on in society. Because of our sinful self-seeking, peace is only achieved by subordinating the private purposes of one to others.[19]

The great American social ethicist Reinhold Niebuhr, himself belonging to the Augustinian theological tradition like the one I have been offering, made a similar point. He recognized the importance of having this sort of realism that comes from knowing you are a brave sinner. He put it this way once in a 1960 sermon: "We know, however, that business and politics are not governed by unselfishness." We are always sinning, Niebuhr adds. The best we can hope to attain in society is a balance of power "in order to prevent the strong from taking advantage of the weak, by making the weak a little stronger but not too strong." Martin Luther advocated for this sort of realism, even to the point of contending that it is idolatry if we assume that the people with whom we interact in society are honest.[20]

Elsewhere, elaborating on these points, Niebuhr cynically and realistically added that coercion is involved in politics, even if it is done by peaceful means.[21] Because, since the Fall into sin we are innately selfish, nobody, not even you and me, renounces our privileges freely. That's why we need to be made (at least through certain incentives) to renounce them. Brave sinners are realistic about their politics, realistic about life.

Brave sinners, in contrast to certain strands of Christian belief that have been influenced by the suppositions of Revivalism like Rick Warren has been, know that because sin is everywhere, even in their good deeds, they need to be ready to get their hands dirty by immersing themselves in the trade-offs and self-interest agendas that must transpire in politics. If practiced consistently, the lifestyle of brave sinning entails political engagement, but in such a way that you are open to the messiest compromises you might need to make in order to get the job done. Brave sinners are not so idealistic as to let commitments to pure ideals impede progress.

I do not just want to pick on Warren and those segments of Christianity influenced by the Revivalist-amended strands of the Puritan paradigm. The Catholic Church and mainline Protestant denominations issue impressive social statements advocating justice, and various liberation theologians regularly write books about a preferential option for the poor.[22] That is to say, they believe that God and the Church would have us favor the poor over the rich in ordinary dealings with the world. But at least since the Reagan Revolution in American politics, none of these leaders or agencies has lobbied very effectively for these convictions, engaging instead in the hardball politics that these religious bodies or their predecessors did in helping America to support the labor union movement, as well as to secure women and African Americans the right to vote.

The problem with these church leaders and denominations is that they prefer fidelity to their ideals to the compromises it takes to get things done politically. They are too cowardly in their sinning, failing to recognize that everybody's ideals are twisted by self-serving egocentricity and so are already contaminated. Such good people (pretended sinners) think they can avoid sin, and so try to stay away from what might contaminate them. As it is said in the African-American church, these folks are so holy as to be of no earthly (political) use.

In fact the U.S. Constitution itself presupposes this appreciation of the dirty, self-interested character of politics and human nature. I previously mentioned that America's Founders held these commitments. Among just a few of many examples include James Madison's warning about factions which emerge in society that aim to establish their own self-interest at the expense of everyone else, his warning that majorities can unite around common interests to endanger the rights of the minority, Benjamin Franklin's belief that men are driven by "ambition and avarice," and Alexander Hamilton's contention that "men love power."[23] Given these realities, it was inevitable in the views of these Founders that sometimes you have to give up your ideals or what you want for the sake of the common good. Madison claimed that delegates to the Constitutional Convention were "compelled to sacrifice theoretical propriety to the force of extraneous considerations." Generalizing to all political decisions, Hamilton observed: "I never expect to see a perfect work from imperfect man. The result of the deliberations of all collective bodies must necessarily be a compound, as well of the errors and prejudices as of the good sense and wisdom of the individuals of whom they are composed."[24]

Brave sinners are more comfortable with their own fallibility. As a result, they can more readily engage in the compromises it takes to make politics for the common good happen.

To believe in the fallen nature of humanity, our innate selfishness, entails that we cannot trust the free market to monitor itself. An awareness of our sin (especially among brave sinners) leads to a belief in the need to redistribute wealth and power. Of course this is contrary to what many Americans think (largely as a result of quality marketing by the Right). The media has lured us into thinking that the American system supports the free market. Not so, when we consider the thinking of Madison and Hamilton, as the quotes below indicate. Others could be cited:

> [T]he great object should be to combat the evil [of faction] . . . By withholding *unnecessary* opportunities from a few. . . . By the silent operation of laws, which, without violating the rights of property, reduce extreme wealth towards a state of mediocrity, and raise extreme indigence towards a state of comfort.[25]
>
> Happy it is when the interest which the government has in the preservation of its own power coincides with a proper distribution of the public burdens and trend to guard the least wealthy part of the community from oppression.[26]

If we could nurture this Constitutional awareness of our sinfulness and corresponding need for programs which redistribute some of our wealth, a lot of America's problems we have been noting regarding poverty, health insurance, and upward social mobility might be more readily addressed. Failures in the market at the end of the Bush era, mandating federal government financial bailouts, have indicated that realistic politics must include openness to government managing the economy. But because of our selfishness, greed, and blind desire for power, it still won't be easy to get the legislation actually to redistribute wealth. Good to know America's Founders approved.

This sort of renunciation of power and wealth for the sake of the common good comes a little easier for brave sinners. Rebellious as they are, as I have already noted, they cannot abide the injustice, evil, and death that surrounds us. They are less likely to take the acquisition of power too seriously, to regard the trappings of politics and wealth as mere play. As I previously observed, over 1,500 years ago Augustine made this point, contending that the idleness of play is similar to what elders call business.[27] When you understand life as play, then your possessions, the admiration others have for you, your accomplishments, and your influence will not matter as much. The accumulation of such things has no more importance than winning a game. Rebelliously renouncing these for the sake of those in need matters a lot less for brave sinners who see life as play. After all, to give away a few sandlot baseball homeruns or Internet games or chess victories is no big deal. To see life as play, as brave sinners do, makes it a lot more fun.

THE LIFE OF BRAVE SINNING

We have seen what a just society might look like, how the lifestyle of brave sinning can make a difference to American society. But what would it be like for you as an individual to live as a brave sinner? What does it feel like to have the dopamine and serotonin flood your frontal lobe, as is likely to transpire for the brave sinner? Martin Luther described this feeling of total dependence on God's grace, of being flooded with this ecstasy. In his view it is like being drunk.[28] When you're drunk (especially when it is drunk with God), you are having fun.

Elsewhere Luther elaborated on the joy of brave sinning. For the Christian, he claimed, nothing is vexatious or troubling:

> The life of such a person and whatever he does, whether great or small and no matter what it is called, is nothing by fruit and cannot be without fruit. . . . Everything such a person does comes easy for him, not troublesome or

vexatious. Nothing is too arduous for him or too difficult to suffer and bear.[29]

Good works are not troubling, Luther claims elsewhere, because brave sinners understand that they don't have to do them. Brave sinners know that they get no points with God for doing good deeds since all that they do remains mired in sin. As a result the good that is done by them is God's work making good out of the fallible, all-too-egocentric things that they do. When you're a brave sinner, you are no longer caught up in what you are doing, but focused on the transcendent reality bigger than you are (God) who makes good out of what you do.

We have seen that cutting-edge Medical Science research has shown that the front part of the brain gets more active when you forget yourself to concentrate on God and bigger projects like brave sinners do. When that happens, the happiness chemicals (dopamine and serotonin) get secreted in the brain's left prefrontal cortex. We are reminded again that even concentrating on God since the Fall into sin is itself an activity mired in self-seeking pleasure and so marred by sin. Yet such a life, devoted to God as it is, is not to be rejected. It is in fact the bravest of all sins. Such brave sinning leads to a life of service to others and fun.[30]

Early in the Reformation, Martin Luther made an observation about the life of brave sinning that echoes my hypothesis:

> . . . if someone desires from me a service, I can render him,
> I will gladly do it out of goodwill. . . . All our works should
> be of such a nature that they flow from pleasure and love . . .
> since for ourselves we need nothing to make us pious.[31]

Brave sinning is surely good medicine for a society addicted to drugs and the highs resulting from wealth, power, influence, accumulation of the latest trinkets, and celebrity. Who needs those artificial highs when God (through our natural brain chemicals) is giving you this life of joy through participation in the big projects of life?

Of course this joy is not naive and "Pollyannaish." In a paradoxical way, there is something very freeing, even comforting and inspiring, in becoming realistic about human motives, in bravely recognizing that in all that we do, even in our good deeds, human beings are seeking (sometimes frantically) self-fulfillment. Such an insight helps us become more self-critical, more socially and politically alert, and more tolerant of others' foibles. We are also more likely to become more alert to the miracles in life as we marvel that any good can emerge from our sinful, selfish motives. And in our marveling God will use our brain mechanisms to produce more happiness, and in turn even more rebellious courage. I now close with some hints about living this way.

Conclusion

Sin Bravely!

Before proceeding to a discussion of some hints for how to sin bravely, let's review why it matters. I've examined American Christianity's historic infatuation with a duty-oriented conception of faith. In this context, I have demonstrated that the impact of Rick Warren's purpose-driven vision of life as well as the Prosperity Gospel make perfect sense. Both make clear that we have certain obligations to God in order to find our purpose or to prosper. Indeed, both of those significant spiritual options flirt with the ancient heresy of Pelagianism. And their affinities with core suppositions of American spirituality entail such a close relationship between them and Warren's as well as the Prosperity Gospel's view that these theological alternatives stand little realistic chance of effectively critiquing core American social-cultural suppositions.

A stress on what we are to do, as Warren and Prosperity Gospel colleagues advocate, can lead to guilt or to a preoccupation without ourselves, and not with God. Contrary to good intentions, faith on these grounds can easily become primarily about what we can get out of it for ourselves—nurturing a kind of lifestyle readily co-opted by the dominant narcissist ethos of our twenty-first-century context.

I have presented Martin Luther's vision of the Christian life as a life of brave sinning as an alternative to Warren's and the Prosperity Gospel's vision. Preceding chapters have explored this concept more thoroughly than any previous analysis of Luther's thought. It has been shown that the core of brave sinning is the awareness that in all we do (even in our very best, most benevolent and loving behaviors), we are sinning. Such a lifestyle leads to total dependence on God, for brave sinners know that any good accomplished by selfish human beings must in fact be God's work, since selfish people can't do good works on their own.

When we sin bravely in this way we can get our ego out of the way as we recognize that the good we do is actually being done by God through us despite our seedy motives. The awareness leads to freedom and joy, since the pressure is now removed to do and be good. In addition, such total dependence on God entails a self-forgetfulness (not unlike what happens when we fall passionately in love) that leads to happiness.

We've examined both the theological-biblical and scientific reasons for such happiness. With regard to the latter, it has been demonstrated that according to cutting-edge neurobiological research, the more human beings forget themselves and concentrate instead on aims and priorities bigger than they are as individuals (activities like dependence on God), the front part of the brain (the prefrontal cortex) goes into overdrive. And that is the very part of the human brain which when activated revels in pleasurable brain chemicals that produce sensations of contentment and happiness along with high levels of motivation.

This Neurobiological data opens some interesting possibilities for proclaiming Luther's Word of brave sinning to American society as a whole. There is a lot at stake, we have seen. It will take a model like Luther's self-transcendent, joyful, God-centered way of life to change America, to get us away from our self-seeking narcissism and mad chase for self-fulfillment. But how do we get this message out, particularly in view of how Americans have gravitated toward Warren's and the Prosperity Gospel's vision?

Part of the reason for the success of these options, we have seen, is that they feed the therapeutic, self-centered dynamics that dominate contemporary American life. But it has also been observed that Warren's skills in niche marketing facilitate his impact. In order for Martin Luther's vision of brave sinning to have that sort of impact we may need to explore the niche markets that this Word can most effectively target. I can think of at least three: (1) Brave sinning is a concept with resonance for what is left of the countercultural yearnings of the Baby Boomers. (2) The same "middle-finger to the establishment" ethos of Generation Xers taken with rap music, for example, suggests an audience that might be eager to hear a call to brave sinning. (3) Finally for those weighed down by guilt or regret, with disappointment about the turns life has taken (an audience comprised of the Boomers' elders), the Word of freedom and forgiveness that emanates from brave sinning is just right. Speaking of aging, additional research I have undertaken also suggests that there may not just be health advantages to the life of brave sinning. The biological mechanisms set off by such a lifestyle have salubrious implications for impeding the aging process. That is a book for another day.

It may be, though, that we do not need to worry so much about niche marketing, about stroking the theme of countercultural rebelliousness to some audiences and the theme of forgiveness and God-centered spirituality to others. The commonality of our neurological functioning may render this sort of marketing less essential. Maybe all the Church and the academy need to do is help everyone see the connections between brave sinning and happy brain functions, how a spirituality totally dependent on

God because we have renounced a sense that we have earned our own privileges leads to happiness and fulfillment. Of course to that insight it is crucial to add that you won't have such pleasurable, meaningful experiences if your focus is on finding happiness, purpose, and prosperity. We have seen that these good things of life only happen with a life of renunciation of self; their likelihood is more enhanced with a life of brave sinning.

How can we get these highs, become brave sinners? In a sense, brave sinners contend, there is no formula. Indeed, if you try to have a formula to achieve happiness or meaning in life you are becoming so preoccupied with yourself and your own agenda that you will not enjoy all the salubrious consequences that accompany an active prefrontal cortex. This is what happens when our lives are purpose driven or focused on prosperity. We become a bit too preoccupied with our own context and agenda to dim the activities of the back part of the brain, to enjoy the full flow of dopamine in the front part of our brains.

No, there isn't a magic formula or how-to rubric for practicing a life of brave sinning. Martin Luther taught us that because of humanity's saturation with sin the Christian life's ways are hidden from the world.[1] Besides, brave sinners are free from the Law (Galatians 3:10–14). Each of us is set free to sin bravely in our own way. With all his prescriptions on what purpose-driven living looks like, Rick Warren and Prosperity Gospel preaching forfeit Christian freedom. Martin Luther and I won't do this to you. But at least I can offer some practical hints to help you look at your life as a brave sinner.

HOW BRAVE SINNING MIGHT BE
EXPERIENCED IN YOUR LIFE

Freedom from the Law entails that my way of being a rebel, glorifying God, and serving others isn't your way. As Christians, the way both of us rebel, glorify God, and serve will not be admired by the world. So follow your dreams and your yearnings, not the world's agenda. Play your own favorite games of life, follow your own vision of what makes life worth living. Follow your own vision of how to rebel against the meaninglessness of life. But at least in closing I can help us all start to live lives of brave sinning by raising several questions for you to consider and implement in everyday life.

1. Are you ready to concede that for every activity in which you participate, even those which receive your best intentions, you are engaging in them because they feel good or at least put off pain? If so, then you can start to see how selfishness and sin mar all you do. If not, face the music: you are a coward(-ly sinner). But remember that people who do not believe they are sinners in all they do are so sufficiently pleased with themselves that they are likely to keep on doing what they've always done. In this case, you will not likely experience much more joy than you presently have. (Perhaps you'll begin to experience even less joy, because after dopamine saturates the same neurons for a while, just like any drug, the parts of our bodies exposed to it begin building an immunity that reduces the effects of the chemical high.) You certainly will not change the world if you keep on doing what you have always done.

2. Write down a handful of things for which you yearn. Try to recall what you wanted to do with your life when you were young. Keep in mind, though, that brave sinners are not cowardly about their sins. If the yearning and dreams you have are

only about you, what you want, or the approval and admiration of others, what makes you think that you can expect much long-term happiness? Also keep in mind that you want to get the frontal lobes of your brain working. That happens best when you don't fret about purpose or prosperity. It happens best when your hopes and dreams are directed toward projects that are bigger than your own prosperity, self-gratification, or purpose. The bigger the project (and of course doing something for God, the Lord of all being, is the biggest project), then your frontal lobes are activated, so that your whole body is likely to experience those dopamine highs.

3. Be realistic about those dreams. Brave sinners are realistic. They know that in a world full of sinners like us, good ideas and noble aims are not usually realized. Egos and concupiscence frequently get in the way. Consequently it is good to revise your original yearnings in order that they stand a chance to get realized at least in part. Realistic, brave sinners are willing to settle for progress, even if it "ain't the ideal." In the struggle against chaos, injustice, and meaninglessness, something's better than nothing. Also, when you are in dialogue with what's doable, and are willing to adjust, you will likely forge more neural connections, and the more such connections are developed, the more monoamines can saturate the brain's frontal lobe to the pleasure of the whole human body. This process is also good for postponing the aging process. So dream big, but keep revising those dreams to make them work.

4. Is it clear that brave sinning is not about you, not about how you can find prosperity, purpose, or well-being even if your intentions are good? If you are willing to acknowledge that you sin in everything you do, then you will begin to appreciate that you can't find meaning in life on your own. It can only happen as a gift from God, when you are wrapped up in life's

greatest Good which transcends you, in God. Looking at life this way is a lesson in humility, a recognition that all the good you have in life is not your own doing. Brave sinners, aware that their sin precludes their ability truly to do good, recognize that all the good they have in life is God's work. As a result, they are inclined to see life through the lens of the miraculous and with awe. Try looking at life not as humdrum and natural, but as a manifestation of impossible dreams. A good job and nice families really are miraculous. And as for the comforts of twenty-first-century American life, they are far beyond what our forebears in the early 1900s could have dreamed or imagined. When you see sin in all you do, the awareness of the undeserved, miraculous character of the good you have emerges spontaneously.

5. Looking at everyday events as play can make your life a lot more fun. Don't make them such a serious matter. Focus on the enjoyable parts of your work, the people with whom you interact (even the weirdos, who are worth a laugh). Isn't living together or raising children fun, too? Learning from youth as well as being aware of our sin teach us this lesson. Children teach us valuable lessons for living the Christian life, for living life with joy as play, for not taking ourselves and our importance too seriously, for living the way Jesus Christ wants us to live (Matthew 19:14; Mark 10:14–15; Luke 18:17). As sinners, since we can't do anything but sin, bringing good into the world must be God's act. Preserving the world does not depend on you and me, and God's shoulders are certainly broad enough to get the job done. So let's enjoy life; see it as play. When you understand life as play, then your possessions, the admiration others have for you, your accomplishments, and your influence will not matter as much. In the midst of play you forget yourself, and when that happens, the frontal lobe of your brain goes into high gear along with all the pleasure that it brings.

The sort of self-examination I am trying to encourage with these questions and reflections is not agonizing. That's the problem with a lot of self-help visions, including Warren's or the Prosperity Gospel's, that promise happiness, purpose, or prosperity if you follow their prescriptions. No promises to brave sinners from my end. Happiness is out of our hands if you believe as Luther does, but this insight removes the pressure and agony about finding joy and meaning in life. It is only by the grace of God, thanks to God's Word of forgiving love that never abandons us, that brave sinners have a lot more fun when discerning purpose and meaning in life.

So sin bravely! But believe and rejoice in Christ even more bravely. "As long as we are here [in this world] we have to sin. . . . [But n]o sin will separate us" from Christ.[2] Have fun, too.

NOTES

INTRODUCTION

1. For the assessment as a consensus among many observers, see Sonja Steptoe, "The Man with the Purpose," *Time*, March 29, 2004, 54.

2. Wade Clark Roof, *Spiritual Marketplace: Baby Boomers and the Remaking of American Religion*, reported in Steptoe, 55. For a friendlier assessment, see Douglas B. Sosnik, Matthew J. Dowd, and Ron Fournier, *Applebee's America: How Successful Political, Business, and Religious Leaders Connect with the New American Community* (New York: Simon & Schuster, 2006), 102–15.

3. Rick Warren, *The Purpose Driven Life* (Grand Rapids, MI: Zondervan, 2002), esp. 17–18.

4. Sydney E. Ahlstrom, *A Religious History of the American People* (New Haven, CT: Yale University Press, 1972), 3, 12, 1079, 1094–96; H. Richard Niebuhr, *The Kingdom of God in America* (New York: Harper & Row, 1937), esp. 8, 45ff.; Mark Noll, "The Luther Difference," *First Things*, February 1992, 38.

5. Augustine, *De spiritu et littera* (412), III.5–IV.6; II.3–4, in *Nicene and Post-Nicene Fathers*, ed. Philip Schaff, First Series, Vol. 5 (reprint ed.; 2nd print.; Peabody, MA: Hendrickson, 1995), 84–85.

6. Luther makes these points in his *Letter to Philip Melanchthon* (1521), in *D. Martin Luthers Werke*, Kritische Gesamtausgabe, Briefwechsel (15 vols.; Weimar, Germany: Hermann Bohlaus Nachfolger, 1930ff.), Vol. 2, 372, l. 84/English translation in

Luther's Works, Vol. 48, ed. Gottfried Krodel (Philadelphia: Fortress Press, 1963), 281–82; Martin Luther, *Evangelium am elsten Sonntage nach Trinitatis*, in *Crucigers Sommerpostille* (1543 ed.), in *D. Martin Luthers Werke*, Kritische Gesamtausgabe (Weimar Ausgabe), Vol. 22 (65 vols.; Weimar, Germany: Hermann Bohlaus Nachfolger, 1883ff.), 210f., ll.16ff. / English translation in *Sermons of Martin Luther*, Vol. 4, trans. and ed. Nicholas John Lenker (reprint ed.; Grand Rapids, MI: Baker, 1988), 367–68.

CHAPTER 1
Rick Warren and American Christianity

1. For this analysis I am indebted to Douglas B. Sosnik, Matthew J. Dowd, and Ron Fournier, *Applebee's America: How Successful Political, Business, and Religious Leaders Connect with the North American Community* (New York: Simon & Schuster, 2006), esp. 93–126.

2. Rick Warren, as quoted in ibid., 118.

3. Ibid., 5–6, 7, 82–83, 95, 126, 180–97.

4. Rick Warren, *The Purpose Driven Life: What on Earth Am I Here For?* (Grand Rapids, MI: Zondervan, 2002), 17.

5. Ibid., 17–18; Rick Warren, *God's Answers to Life's Difficult Questions* (Grand Rapids, MI: Zondervan, 2006), 46–48.

6. Warren, as quoted in Sosnik et al., *Applebee's America*, 118.

7. See Christopher Lasch, *The Culture of Narcissism: American Life in an Age of Diminishing Expectations* (New York: W. W. Norton & Co., 1979).

8. For these statistics, see John Fetto, "What Seems to Be the Problem?" in *American Demographics*, April 1, 2002, at http://find articles.com/p/articles/mi_m4021/is_ai_87109755 [accessed November 26, 2008].

9. The survey noted was undertaken by the National Opinion Research Center, and was reported in *USA Today*, June 22, 2006, at USATODAY.com. For this assessment of the impact of Narcissism in Western Europe, see Bernard Cova, "The Tribalisation of Society and Its Impact on the Conduct of Marketing" (2002), at http://visionary marketing.com/articles/cova/cova-tribe-2001 [accessed November 26, 2008].

10. Statistics available in Kevin A. Hassett and Aparna Mathuu, "Conspicuous Consumption," in National Review Online, at http:// nrd.national review.com/article [accessed November 26, 2008].

11. For these statistics, see www.scribd.com/doc/1678034/ TransportationStatistics [accessed November 26, 2008]; F. Weller, "Economic Snapshot for November 2008, at http://www.american progress.org/issues/2008/11 [accessed November 26, 2008]; and Christian E. Weller, "Drowning in Debt," at http://www.american progress.org/issues/2006/05 [accessed November 26, 2008].

12. See Sarah Roberts, "Survey Confirms that Americans are Overworked, Overspent, and Rethinking the American Dream," at http://www.newdream.org/newsletter/survey.php [accessed November 26, 2008]. For the more recent Gallup poll, see "Republicans Sour on Nation's Moral Climate," June 12, 2008, at http://www.gallup.com/ poll/107881/Republicans-Sour-Nations-Moral-Climate.aspx?version [accessed November 26, 2008].

13. For these insights I am indebted to Christine Rosen, "The Overpraised American," *Policy Review* (October & November 2005), at http://www.questia.com/PM.qst;;sessionid [accessed November 26, 2008].

14. U.S. Census Bureau news, Feb. 8, 2002, at http://www.census. gov/PressRelease [accessed May 14, 2008]; Barna Research Group, "Morality Continues to Decay" (2003); see the report of another Barna Study in Hannah Elliot, "Sex: Younger generation accepts Boomer experimentation as normal" (2006); Jane Lampmon, "Poll: Americans More Accepting," *Christian Science Monitor*, October 24, 2005.

15. U.S. Department of Education, National Center for Education Statistics (2005), reported at http://www.childstats.gov/americas children/famsoc3.asp [accessed November 26, 2008].

16. See Rosen, "The Overpriced American," for these statistics.

17. Reported in Ibid.

18. Warren, *The Purpose Driven Life*, 73.

19. See ibid., 7–8, for a summary of these purposes.

20. Ibid., 261.

21. Ibid., 30–33.

22. Ibid., 95; cf. Philip Melanchthon, *Confessio Augustana* (1530), XX.27. English translation in *The Book of Concord*, ed. Robert Kolb and Timothy Wengert (Minneapolis: Fortress Press, 2000), 56.

124   *Sin Bravely*

23. See Warren, *The Purpose Driven Life*, 318–19, for his discussion of being of use to God.

24. Ibid., 283, 179; Saddleback Valley Community Church, "Membership Covenant."

25. Warren, *The Purpose Driven Life*, 191; cf. 92, 95, 97.

26. Ibid., 252–55.

27. Ibid., 174; Rick Warren, *The Purpose of Christmas* (New York: Howard Books, 2008), 51–53, 56–58, 68, 69, 80–82; Rick Warren, "Keynote Speech" (at the Martin Luther King, Jr. Annual Commemorative Service, Atlanta, GA, January 19, 2009), cf. Warren, *God's Answers to Life's Difficult Questions*, 34–37.

28. For the first of these commitments, see Warren, *The Purpose Driven Life*, 167.

29. Ibid., 153.

30. Ibid., 262, 232, 194–95; Warren, *God's Answers to Life's Difficult Questions*, 140; cf. 183–84, 195; Warren, *The Purpose of Christmas*, 58; Joel Osteen, *Your Best Life Now* (New York: Faith Words, 2004), 32, 38; Joel Osteen, *Become a Better You* (New York: The Free Press, 2007), 366, 5.

31. Martin Luther, *Auslegung des dritten und vierten Kapitels Johannis* (1538), XXXII, in *D. Martin Luthers Werke*, Kritische Gesamtausgabe (Weimar Ausgabe), Vol. 47 (65 vols.; Weimar, Germany: Hermann Bohlaus Nachfolger, 1883ff.), 98ff., ll.17ff. [hereafter referred to as WA]/English translation in *Luther's Works*, Vol. 22, (54 vols; St. Louis—Philadelphia: Concordia Publishing House—Fortress Press, 1955ff.), 375ff. [hereafter referred to as LW]; Martin Luther, *Epistel Messe in der Christenacht*, 44–45, in *Kirchenpostille 1522*, WA 10^{I/1}: 44f., 13ff./English translation in *Sermons of Martin Luther*, Vol. VI, ed. and trans. John Nicholas Lenker (Grand Rapids, MI: Baker Books, 1988), 135–36.

32. Warren, *The Purpose Driven Life*, 205, 260, 272–78.

33. *Formulae Concordiae* (1577), SD VI.22/English translation in *The Book of Concord*, 591.

34. Warren, *The Purpose Driven Life*, 109.

35. Ibid., 281.

36. Augustine, *In Joannis evangelium tractatus* (c.416), XXXI.5, in *Nicene and Post-Nicene Fathers*, ed. Philip Schaff, First Series, Vol. 7 (reprint ed.; 2nd print.; Peabody, MA: Hendrickson, 1995), 190; Martin Luther, *Die ander Epistel S. Petri ein S. Judas gepiedigt und*

asgelest (1523/1524), WA14: 70f., 27ff./LW 30:196; John Calvin, *Instiutio Religionis Christianae* (1559), III.XXI.5/English translation, ed. John T. McNeill (Philadelphia: Westminster Press, 1967), 926; cf. Alsber Einstein, "Zur Elektrodynamik bewegter Korper," *Analen der Physik* 17 (1905): 891–921.

37. Warren, *The Purpose Driven Life*, 212.

38. Gabriel Biel, *The Circumcision of the Lord* (n.d.)/English translation in *Forerunners of the Reformation*, ed. Heiko Oberman (Philadelphia: Fortress Press, 1966), 173; Martin Luther, *Disputatio Heidlebergae habita* (1518), Cor.18, WA1:137,6/LW31:67. Cf. Osteen, *Your Best Life Now*, 20, 22, 43.

39. Warren, *The Purpose Driven Life*, 220; Warren, *God's Answers to Life's Difficult Questions*, 59, 114, 133–34, 146–49.

40. Sydney E. Ahlstrom, *A Religious History of the American People* (New Haven, CT: Yale University Press, 1972), 3, 12, 1079, 1094–96; H. Richard Niebuhr, *The Kingdom of God in America* (New York: Harper & Row, 1937), esp. 8, 45ff.; Mark Noll, "The Luther Difference," *First Things*, February 1992, 38; Mark Ellingsen, *When Did Jesus Become Republican? Rescuing Our Country and Our Values from the Right* (Lanham, MD: Rowman & Littlefield, 2007), 11ff.

41. *The Westminster Confession* (1646), V.1; III.

42. Ibid., XVIII.2; XXI.5.

43. *Reliquiae Baxterianae; or Mr. Richard Baxter's Narrative of the Most Memorable Passages of His Life and Times* (1696), 30; Richard Steele, *The Tradesman's Calling, Being a Discourse Concerning the Nature, Necessity, Choice, etc., of a Calling in General* (1684), 22.

44. I develop the implications of the Puritan Paradigm for contemporary American politics more fully in *When Did Jesus Become Republican?*

45. Barna Research Group, "Religious Beliefs Vary Widely By Denomination" (2001), at http://www.barna.org/FlexPage.aspx?Page=BarnaUpdate&BarnaUpdateID=92 [accessed December 17, 2001].

46. *The Westminster Confession*, I; XXI; XXIII; XXVII–XXIX; cf. Pew Forum on Religion & Public Life, "Many Americans Uneasy with Mix of Religion and Politics" (2006), at http://pewforum.org/docs/index.php?/DocID=153 [accessed November 26, 2008]; Pew Forum on Religion in Public Life, "More Americans Question Religion's Role in Politics" (2008), at http://pewforum.org/docs/?DocID=334 [accessed November 26, 2008].

47. *The Westminster Confession*, VI.

48. John Witherspoon, *An Annotated Edition of Lectures on Moral Philosophy*, ed. Jack Scott (Newark: University of Delaware Press, 1982), 144; James Madison, "No. 10," "No. 51," in *The Federalist Papers* (New York: Mentor, 1961), 77–84, 324–25; Alexander Hamilton, "No. 71," in *The Federalist Papers*, 432. For a similar assessment, see John Eidsmoe, *Christianity and the Constitution: The Faith of Our Founding Fathers* (Grand Rapids, MI: Baker Books, 1987), esp. 88, 101, 146–47, 340–42, 369–72. As we will see in chapter 6, Madison and many of the Founders believed human beings were driven by self-interest and selfishness (sin). This could often lead to efforts to gain advantage for oneself and one's friends at the expense of the common good. The only way to remedy this, the Founders came to believe, was by sharing power, through the separation of government power in three branches.

49. Barna Research Group, "Religious Beliefs Vary Widely By Denomination," *New York Times Magazine*, May 7, 2000. Also, see note 45.

50. Compare *The Westminster Confession of Faith* to the teaching of early Baptist Confessions of Faith like the *Second London Confession* (1677/1688), I, III, V.1, X.1, XIX.4–6, XXIV.2; *The New Hampshire Confession* (1833), i, ix, xi, xvi.

51. Dwight Moody, "The Gateway into the Kingdom," in *The Way to God and How to Find It* (Chicago: Moody Press, 1884), 33; Dwight Moody, "Perseverance," in *"To All People"* (New York: E. B. Treat, 1877), 166; Billy Sunday, quoted in Edwin S. Gaustad, ed., *A Documentary History of Religion in America Since 1965* (Grand Rapids, MI: Eerdmans, 1993), 291; Billy Graham, *The Holy Spirit* (Waco, TX: Warner Books, 1978), 13–14, 160ff.

52. Barna Research Group, "Beliefs: General Religious" (2007), at http://www.barna.orgFlexPage.aspx?Page=Topic&TopicID=2 [accessed November 27, 2008]. For Warren's affirmation of this commitments, see *The Purpose Driven Life*, 262, 232, 194–95; Warren, *God's Answers to Life's Difficult Questions*, 140; cf. ibid., 183–84, 195; Warren, *The Purpose of Christmas*, 58; Joel Osteen, *Your Best Life Now* (New York: Faith Words, 2004), 32, 38; Joel Osteen, *Become a Better You* (New York: The Free Press, 2007), 366, 5.

53. For data on contemporary American attitudes toward human nature, see Barna Research Group, "Religious Beliefs Vary Widely

by Denomination." For indication of the endorsement of deism by some of the Founders, see Thomas Jefferson, "Letter to Dr. Benjamin Waterhouse" (1822), in *Writings* (New York: Library of America, 1984), 1458–59; Benjamin Franklin, "On the Providence of God in the Government of the World," *Writings* (New York: Library of America, 1987), 165–68. For a detailed discussion of the Secular-Democratic strand of the American political system (especially evident in the Declaration of Independence) in relation to the realism about human nature embedded in the Constitution, see Mark Ellingsen, *Blessed Are the Cynical: How Original Sin Can Make America a Better Place* (Grand Rapids, MI: Brazos Press, 2003), esp. 51–67.

54. Dwight Moody, "The Gateway into the Kingdom," in *The Way to God and How to Find It* (Chicago: Moody Press, 1884), 23; Dwight Moody, "Come," in *Great Joy* (New York: E. B. Treat, 1877), esp. 492; Dwight Moody, "Coming to Christ," in *"To All People,"* 155–57; Sunday, quoted in Gaustad, *A Documentary History of Religion in America Since 1965*, 291. Consider the central role of the altar call in Billy Graham's revivals.

55. Dwight Moody, as quoted in William G. McLoughlin Jr., *Modern Revivalism: Charles Grandison Finney to Billy Graham* (New York: Ronald Press Co., 1959), 277; Dwight Moody, "The Workingman and His Foes," *Christian Advocate*, March 4, 1875, 68; Billy Sunday, as quoted in the *Boston Herald*, December 14, 1916, 5, January 12, 1917, 3; Billy Sunday, as quoted in *The New York Times*, May 20, 1916, 5; Billy Graham, "Why Lausanne?" *Christianity Today*, September 13, 1974, 12; Billy Graham, "What Ten Years Have Taught Me," *The Christian Century*, February 17, 1960, 187, 188.

For the social concerns of the Great Awakenings, see Jonathan Edwards, *Christian Charity; or, The Duty of Christ to the Poor, Explained and Enforced* (n.d.), IIff., in *Works*, Vol. 2 (Peabody, MA: Hendrickson, 1998), 164–73; Charles G. Finney, *Lectures on Revivals* (New York, 1835), 265–66, 271.

56. See Ellingsen, *When Did Jesus Become Republican?* for a detailed discussion of these dynamics.

57. Warren, *The Purpose Driven Life*, 120–21.

58. Ibid., 117–67.

59. Ibid., 123–24. This sort of exegesis on Warren's part is typical of his exegetical approach. To say the least, his use of various biblical translations and quoting of only a portion of some biblical verses,

with little attention to their context (ibid., 325), is questionable exegetical work.

60. Ibid., 283–84.

61. P.E.A.C.E.: Promote reconciliation, Equip leaders, Assist the poor, Care for the sick, Educate the next generation.

62. Rick Warren, "The ONE Campaign: An Advocacy Letter from Rick Warren" (June 3, 2005); Warren, "Keynote Speech."

63. "Pastor Rick's News & Views 10/23/2008 Part 3 (Prop 8)," at http://www.saddlebackfamily.com/blogs/newsandviews/index/html? contentid [accessed December 22, 2008]. For references to both Warren's and Osteen's positions on homosexuality as sin, see the quotations in Marc Gunther, "Will Success Spoil Rick Warren?" *Fortune* (October 31, 2005), at http://money.cnn.com/magazines/fortune/fortune_archive/2005/10/31/8359189/index.htm [accessed December 19, 2008]; Lillian Kwon, "Joel Osteen maintains homosexuality is sin," *Christian Today* (May 14, 2008), at http://www.christiantoday.com/articledir/print.htm?id=18763 [accessed December 19, 2008]. For Warren's denunciation of gay marriage, see "Rick Warren's Controversial Comments on Gay Marriage," *Beliefnet* (December 17, 2008), at http://blog.beliefnet.com/stevenwaldman/2008/12/rick-warrens-controversial-com.html [accessed December 20, 2008]. In the heat of the controversy caused by these statements, the website for Warren's Saddleback Church which had stated that unrepentant practicing gays would not be accepted as members (http://www.saddlebackfamily.com/home/whatwebelieve [accessed December 19, 2008]) was changed by December 22, deleting this membership stipulation.

CHAPTER 2

How Purpose-Driven Living Can Lead to
a Life That's All about You

1. For commentary on these characteristics of our new global economy, see Thomas Friedman, *The World Is Flat: A Brief History of the Twenty-First Century* (paperback ed.; New York: Pacidor/Farrar, Straus and Giroux, 2007), 320, 608–9, 634–35.

2. See Richard Sennett, *The Corrosion of Character: The Personal Consequences of Work in the New Capitalism* (New York: T & T Clark, 1998), 87; for our consumption trends, see statistics cited on p. 123, nn.10–11.

3. For these observations I remain indebted to Christopher Lasch, *The Culture of Narcissism: American Life in an Age of Diminishing Expectations* (New York: W. W. Norton & Co., 1979), 55–58.

4. For these observations I am indebted to Sennett, *The Corrosion of Character*, 74–75.

5. Lasch, *The Culture of Narcissism*, esp. 130–31.

6. Sennett, *The Corrosion of Character*, 48.

7. See ibid., 116–17; Lasch, *The Culture of Narcissism*, 122–23.

8. The most compelling statement of the impact of this mode of thought on the American university and its related institutions has been offered by Allan Bloom, *The Closing of the American Mind: How Higher Education Has Failed Democracy and Impoverished the Souls of Today's Students* (New York: Simon and Schuster, 1987), esp. 141ff.

9. *Reliquiae Baxterianae; or, Mr. Richard Baxter's Narrative of the Most Memorable Passages of His Life and Times* (1696), 30; Richard Steele, *The Tradesman's Calling, Being a Discourse Concerning the Nature, Necessity, Choice, etc., of a Calling in General* (1684), 22; Cotton Mather, *Magnalia Christi Americana*, Vol. 1 (1702; repr., Hartford, 1853), 61.

For a more detailed discussion of the free-market dispositions of these movements, see Mark Ellingsen, *When Did Jesus Become Republican? Rescuing Our Country and Our Values from the Right* (Lanham, MD: Rowman & Littlefield, 2007), 14ff.

10. Dwight Moody, quoted in *Boston Daily Advertiser*, February 12, 1877, 4; Dwight Moody, *The Great Redemption* (Chicago: Merchants' Specialty Co.), 355–56; Billy Sunday, quoted in William G. McLoughlin Jr., *Modern Revivalism: Charles Grandison Finney to Billy Graham* (New York: Ronald Press, 1959), 435.

11. See Billy Graham, "God's Revolutionary Demand," *Christianity Today*, July 21, 1967, 3–5; Billy Graham, *The Challenge* (Garden City, NY: Doubleday, 1969), 71, 126–27.

12. Dwight Moody, *The Way to God and How to Find It* (Chicago: Moody Press, 1884), 23; Billy Sunday, quoted in *Boston Herald*, December 14, 1918, 12; January 12, 1917, 3.

13. For detailed discussion and documentation of these points, see Ellingsen, *When Did Jesus Become Republican?*

14. These insights were inspired by Mark Noll, "The Lutheran Difference," *First Things*, February 1992. For the Arminianism of Revivalism, see Moody, "The Gateway into the Kingdom," in *The Way to God and How to Find It*, 33; Billy Sunday, quoted in Edwin S.

Gaustad, ed., *A Documentary History of Religion in America Since 1865* (Grand Rapids, MI: Eerdmans, 1993), 291. For the Puritan affirmation of the sovereignty of God, see *The Westminster Confession of Faith* (1647), V.

15. Joel Osteen, *Your Best Life Now* (New York: Faith Words, 2004), 24–25, 86–87, 221.

16. Rick Warren, *The Purpose Driven Life* (Grand Rapids, MI: Zondervan, 2002), 17–20, 21, 30–35, 100–106; Rick Warren, *God's Answers to Life's Difficult Questions* (Grand Rapids, MI: Zondervan, 2006), 33; Rick Warren, *The Purpose of Christmas* (New York: Howard Books, 2008), 64.

17. Warren, *The Purpose Driven Life*, 283–84.

18. Ibid., 29.

19. Osteen, *Your Best Life Now*, 221, 231.

20. Lisa Miller, "Redefining God," *Wall Street Journal*, April 21, 2000.

21. Friedrich Schleiermacher, *Der christliche Glaube* (1830), 4, 15–16/English translation in *The Christian Faith*, Vol. 1, ed. H.R. Mackintosh and J.S. Stewart (New York and Evanston: Harper & Row, 1963), 12–18, 76–83.

22. Paul Tillich, *Systematic Theology*, Vol. 1 (3 vols. in one; Chicago: University of Chicago Press, 1967), 3–8, 59, 66; Rudolf Bultmann, *Jesus Christ and Mythology* (New York: Charles Scribner's Sons, 1958), 18, 45, 48, 51; Paul Ricoeur, *Essays in Biblical Interpretation*, ed. Lewis Mudge (Philadelphia: Fortress Press, 1980), 108, 143. Two important Catholic theologians embodying these suppositions are Bernard Lonergan (his Transcendental Method), *Theological Investigations*, Vol. IX (New York: Seabury Press, 1972), 28–33, and one of his most famous American admirers, David Tracy (his Method of Critical Correlation), *Blessed Rage for Order* (New York: Seabury Press, 1978), 43–56, 74–75, 84, 134.

James Cone, "Black Theology in American Religion," *Journal of the American Academy of Religion* 53 (December 1985): 768–69; Rosemary Radford Reuther, "Mother Earth and the Megamachine," *Christianity and Crisis* (December 13, 1971): 269–72.

23. For more detailed analysis of these trends, see Mark Ellingsen, *Blessed Are the Cynical: How Original Sin Can Make America a Better Place* (Grand Rapids, MI: Brazos Press, 2003), 119–39; and *When Did Jesus Become Republican?* 71–89.

24. See pp. 16–20, 41, for examples and documentation. For Osteen on sin, see *Your Best Life Now*, esp. 29–36, 174–84.

25. See pp. 22–23, 24, for references.

26. Thomas Jefferson, "Letter to William Green Minford" (1799), in *Writings* (New York: Library of America, 1984), 1064–66. For a more detailed analysis of these strands, see my *Blessed Are the Cynical*, esp. 52–67.

27. For documentation of their legalism at this point, see pp. 16–20, 41. On the Theological Use of the Law, see [Lutheran] *Formulae Concordiae* (1577), VI.

28. Both of these modern leaders aim to portray a beneficent God; see Warren, *The Purpose Driven Life*, 260, 272–78; Osteen, *Your Best Life Now*, 8, 22–23, 231.

29. Osteen, *Your Best Life Now*, 164–66, 235, 256–57.

30. Martin Luther, *In epistolam S. Pauli ad Galatas Commentarias* (1535), in *D. Martin Luthers Werke*, Kritische Gesamtasgabe (Weimar Ausgabe), Vol. 40ᴵ (65 vols.; Weimar, Germany: Hermann Bohlaus Nachfolger, 1883ff.), 481f., ll.26ff. [hereafter referred to as WA]/ English translation in *Luther's Works*, Vol. 26 (54 vols.; St. Louis/ Philadelphia: Concordia Publishing House/Fortress Press, 1955ff.), 310; Martin Luther, *Die zweite Disputation gegen die Antinomer* (1538), WA 39ᴵ: 428, 1.

31. Martin Luther, *Predigt ube I Tim1, 8–11*, in *Predigten des Jahres 1525*, XIX, in WA 17ᴵ: 122f, 23ff. Cf. Augustine, *Epistulae* CXLV (412–13).3, in *Nicene and Post-Nicene Fathers* [hereafter referred to as NPNF], First Series, Vol. 1 (rev. ed.; 14 vols.; Peabody, MA: Hendrickson, 1995), 496.

32. Martin Luther, *Vorlesungen uber 1. Mose* (1538–1539), WA 43:34f., 39ff. / LW3: 223–25; Martin Luther, *Epistel am Neujahstage*, 13, in *Kirchenpostille 1522*, WA10ᴵ/²: 455, 5/English translation in *Sermons of Martin Luther*, Vol. V (rep. ed.; 8 vols; Grand Rapids, MI: Baker Books, 1988), 271–72; Luther, *Galatas Commentarius*, WA40ᴵᴵ: 7f, 31./LW27: 7; ibid., WA40ᴵ: 529, 16/LW26: 345–46.

33. Luther, *Vorlesungen uber 1. Mose* (1535–1536), WA42: 122, 36/LW 1:163: "Dum enim peccatum in opera est, non sentitur, non terret, non mordet, sed blanditur et delectat."

34. Martin Luther, *Predigt am Ostersonntag*, in *Predigten des Jahres 1530*, VII, in WA 32: 46, 28: "Denn rechen dus selb aus, wenn du die sund wilt selb ablegen, hastu nicht allein unrecht an der sund

gethan, sondern auch wilt uber das Christo ynn sein ampt greiffen und spricht: Ich wil Chrisus sein, das ist denn sich mehr unterwunden denn Gott, welchs denn die groste sunde ist. O nicht umb Gotts willen, sondern lasst yhn Chrisum bleiben, lasst yhm sein ampt, Es ist gnug an den andern sunden die wir thun."

35. Augustine, *De civitate dei* (413–26), XIV.3/NPNF 2:273.

36. Augustine, *Confessiones* (397/401), X.III.3/NPNF 1:142.

37. Blaise Pascal, *Pensees* (1662), 70, 15–16/English translation in *Pensées*, trans. A. J. Krailsheimer (Middlesex, UK: Penguin, 1966), 48.

38. Ibid., 24, 78; Augustine, *Confessiones*, X.XXVIII.39; XIII. XX.28/NPNF 1:153, 199.

39. Augustine, *De civitate dei*, /NPNF 1: 6. Augustine, *Enchiridion ad Laurentium de fide spe et caritate* (421/422), 78/NPNF 3:263.

40. Martin Luther, *Bibel=und Bucheinzeichnungen Luthers* (1545), WA48: 10, 3: "Will doch itzt niemand mehr Sünder sein noch unrecht thun. Wo komen denn die Gottlosen, und der so viel her? Es is die ursach, spricht er, Sie heissens rat, klugheit, weisheit, recht und gut alles was sie thun, niemand sols anders nennen noch strassen. So gehets denn nach dem Sprichtwort: Eim jeden gstelt sein weise wol, Darumb die Welt is Karren vol."

CHAPTER 3
An Augustinian Re-Education about Sin

1. Anthony, in *The Sayings of the Desert Fathers*, trans. Benedicta Ward (Kalamazoo, MI: Cistercian Publications, 1975), 1, 3, 33.

2. Matoes, Longinus, and Moses the Negro, in *Sayings of the Desert Fathers*, 2, 7, 9; 2–4; 5; *The Instructions of Commodianus* (240), 64, in *Ante-Nicene Fathers*, Vol. 4, ed. Alexander Roberts and James Donaldson (reprint ed.; 10 vols.; Peabody, MA: Hendrickson, 1995), 215–16 [hereafter referred to as ANF).

3. Athanasius, *De Incarnatione Verbi Dei* (316–318), 5–7, 13–14, 54, in *Nicene and Post-Nicene Fathers*, Second Series, Vol. 4 (reprint ed.; 14 vols.; Peabody, MA: Hendrickson, 1994), 38–40, 43–44, 65–66 [hereafter referred to as NPNF II].

4. Tertullian, *Exhortatione Castitatis* (n.d.), II/ANF 4:51; Cyprian of Carthage, *Epistles* (n.d.), LXIV/LVIII.5/ANF 5:354.

5. Pelagius, *Letter to Demetriaden* (n.d.), 16, in *Documents of the Christian Church*, ed. Henry Bettenson (2nd ed.; London: Oxford

University Press, 1963), 52; Augustine, *Confessiones* (397/401), X.XXIX.40 in *Nicene and Post-Nicene Fathers*, ed. Philip Schaff, First Series, Vol. 1 (reprint ed.; 14 vols.; Peabody, MA: Hendrickson, 1994), 153 [hereafter referred to as NPNF I]: "Da quod jubes, et jube quod vis."

6. Augustine, *Confessiones*, I.V.5ff., X.XXVIII.39/NPNF I, 1:153.

7. Augustine, *De spiritus et littera* (412), III.5/NPNF I, 5:84–85: "nam neque liberam arbitrium quicquam nisi ad peccandum ualet, si latet ueritatis uia; et cum id quod agendum et quo nitendum est coeperit non latere, nisi etiam delectet et ametur, non agitur, non suscipitur, non bene uiuitur."

8. This viewpoint is not inconsistent with Augustine's claim that free will is not denied by asserting grace, that there is a cooperation of grace and works in bringing about salvation, a view articulated in his *De gratia et libero arbitrio* (426/427), I.1; XXVI.43/NPNF I, 5:443–44, 463. But I am not sure it is in fact what he states. See Augustine, *De natura et gratia* (415), XLVI.54/NPNF I, 5:139. The Lutheran church's *Confessio Augustana* (1530), XVIII, does expressly maintain that we have freedom in ordinary daily decisions while, without grace, ever remaining in bondage to sin.

9. Martin Luther, *Die Vorlesung uber den Romerbrief* (1515–1516), in *D. Martin Luthers Werke*, Kritische Gesamtausgabe (Weimar Ausgabe), Vol. 56 (65 vols.; Weimar, Germany: Hermann Bohlaus Nachfolger, 1883ff.), 304, l.25 [hereafter referred to as WA]/English translation in *Luther's Works*, Vol. 25 (54 vols.; St. Louis—Philadelphia: Concordia Publishing House—Fortress Press, 1955ff.), 291 [hereafter referred to as LW]: "Ratio est, Quia Natura nostra vitio primi peccati tam profunda est in seipsam incurua, vt non solum optima dona Dei sibi inflectat ipsisque fruatur (vt patet in Iustitiariis et hipocritis), immo et ipso Deo vtatur ad illa consequenda, Verum etiam hoc ipsum ignoret, Quod tam inique, curue et praue omnia, etiam Deum, propter seipsam querat." Cf. ibid., WA 56: 356,4/LW 25:345.

10. Martin Luther, *Das Magnificat Verdeutscschet und ausgelegt* (1522), WA 7:556, 25/LW 21:309.

11. Augustine, *Confessiones*, VI.XII.22; VI.XV.25; XIII.VII.8/ NPNF I, 1:99, 100, 192; Augustine, *De civitate Dei* (413–426), XIV.15/NPNF 2:274–75.

12. Augustine, *De nuptiis et concupiscentia* (419/420), I.XXI.24–I. XXIII.25/NPNF I, 5:273–74; cf. Augustine, *Ad Simplicianum* (395/396), I.II.20/*Augustine: Earlier Writings*, ed. J. H. S. Burleigh (Philadelphia: Westminster, 1953), 404 [hereafter referred to as AEW].

13. Augustine, *Ad Simplicianum* (396), I.I.10/AEW: 380; Luther, *Romerbriefvorlesungen*, WA 56: 58,7; 281,6; 321,10/LW 25:24,51, 259, 309; Martin Luther, *Disputatio contra scholasticum Theologiam* (1517), 21, WA 1:255,9/ LW31:10; John Calvin, *Institutio Religionis Christianae* (1559), II.I.8/English translation, ed. John T. McNeill (Philadelphia: Westminster Press, 1967).

14. Augustine, *In Epsitulam Johannis ad Parthos tractatus* (ca. 417), VIII.9/NPNF I, 7:510.

15. Luther, *Romerbriefvorlesungen*, WA 56:237,12/LW25:222: "Quia homo non potest, nisi que sua sunt querere et se super omnia diligere. Que est summa omnium vitiorum. Vnde et in bonis et virtutibus tales querunt seipsos, se. Vt sibi placeant et plaudant."

Martin Luther, *Grund unnd ursach aller Artickel D. Mart:. Luther so durch Romische bülle unrechtlich vordampt seyn* (1521), WA 7:445,17/LW 32:91: "Drumb musz ich den Artickel auch widderruffen unnd nu alszo sagen: Es soll niemant dran zweiffelnn, das alle unszer gute werck todsund sein, szo sie nach gottes gericht unnd ernst geurteilt und nit allein aufz gnadenn fur gut angenommen werdenn . . ."

16. Calvin, I.I.2/English translation, 37–38.

17. Martin Luther, *Tischreden* (1531), No. 138, WATR 1:60,26: ". . . de Erbsünde im Menschen wäre gleich wie eines Mannes Bart, welcher, ob er wol heute abgeschnitten würde, dasz einer gar glatt ums Maul wäre, dennoch wüchse ihm der Bart des Morgens wieder. Solches Machsen der Här und Barts hörete nicht auf, dieweil ein Mensch lebte; wenn man aber mit der Schaufel zuschlägt, so hörets auf. Also bleibet der Erbsünde auch in uns und reget sich, dieweil wir leben. . . ."

Cf. Martin Luther, *Passio: Der sechste Predig, in Hauspostille 1545*, WA52:775, 8.

18. Augustine, *Contra Duos Epistolas Pelagianorum* (420), III. VII.20–21/ NPNF I, 5:411–12; cf. Martin Luther, *Enarratio Psalmi LI* (1538), WA 40^{II}:455f., 39/LW 12:400–401; *Apologia Confessionis Augustanae* (1531), XVIII.9.

19. Augustine, *De gratia et libero arbitrio*, iv.8/NPNF I, 5:447; Martin Luther, *Resolutiones Lutheriane super propositionibus suis Lipsiae disputatis* (1519), WA 2:422, 6.

20. Augustine, *De Doctrina Christiana* (397), I.22.20–21; I.33.36/ NPNF I, 2:527–28, 532.

21. For a more detailed sketch of this vision, see Mark Ellingsen, *A Common Sense Theology: The Bible, Faith, and American Society* (Macon, GA: Mercer University Press, 1995), 203–4.

22. Because the greatest mitochondrial DNA variations occur among people of African descent, the oldest line of descent seems likely to have been African. See Allan C. Wilson and Rebecca L. Cann, "The Recent African Genesis of Humans," *Scientific American* (April 1992): 69–71; Christopher Stringer and Robin McKie, *African exodus: The Origins of Modern Humanity* (New York: Henry Holt, 1997).

23. Augustine, *De nuptiis et concupiscentia*, I.XXIV.27/NPNF I, 5:274–75; Augustine, *De gratia Christi et de peccato originali* (418), II.XXXIII.38/NPNF I, 5:250–51; Augustine, *De correptione et gratia* (426/427), XIII.42/NPNF I, 5:489; cf. Cyprian of Carthage, *Epistles* (n.d.), LXIV/LVIII.5/ANF5:354.

24. Karl Barth, *Church Dogmatics*, Vol.I V/1, eds. G. W. Bromiley and T. F. Torrance (Edinburgh: T & T Clark, 1956), 492. It should be noted that Barth himself did not elaborate much on how interaction with other concupiscent beings shapes the sinner's being. In fact, it might be possible to accuse him of reducing the sinful condition to sinful actions. But see ibid., 507, for a mitigating qualification that may exonerate him from that charge.

25. Augustine, *De nuptiis et concupiscentia*, I.XXXV.28; I.XXIII.25/ NPNF I, 5:275, 274; Martin Luther, *Grund und Ursach aller Artikel D. Mart: Luthers so durch Romische Bulle unrechtlich verdammt sind* (1521), WA7:328ff., 10ff.; 359,18/LW32:19–29, 37–38; Martin Luther, *Rationis Latomianae confutatio* (1521), WA 8:58,7/ LW32: 159ff. Also see note 17, above.

26. Augustine, *De nuptiis et concupiscentia*, I.XXIII.25/NPNF I, 5:274.

27. Richard Dawkins, *The Selfish Gene* (2nd ed.; Oxford: Oxford University Press, 1998), esp. 2–3.

28. Edward O. Wilson, *Sociobiology: The New Synthesis* (Cambridge, MA: Harvard University Press, 1975), 4. For a related discussion of this construal of altruism, see Mary Midgley, *Beast and Man: The Roots of Human Nature* (Ithaca, NY: Cornell University Press, 1978), 138, 198–99.

29. For a more detailed discussion of how to continue to affirm the goodness of the Creation, see above, pp. 58, 135, n.21.

Those claiming selfishness is natural include John Polkinghorne, *Reason and Reality: The Relationship between Science and Theology* (Philadelphia: Trinity Press International, 1991), 99–100; Patricia A. Williams, *Doing without Adam and Eve: Sociobiology and Original Sin* (Minneapolis: Fortress, 2001). Among those contending that sin is not genetically determined include, Susan Brooks Thistlethwaite, "A Gene for Violence? Genetic Determinism and Sin," in Susan Brooks Thistlethwaite, ed., *Adam, Eve and the Genome: The Human Genome Project and Theology* (Minneapolis: Fortress, 2003), 148ff.; Donald T. Campbell, "The Conflict between Social and Biological Evolution and the Concept of Original Sin," *Zygon: Journal of Religion and Science* 10 (1975): 243.

CHAPTER 4
An Introduction to Brave Sinning

1. *The Shorter Catechism* (1646), Q1.

2. Martin Luther, *In epistolam S. Pauli ad Galatas Commentrius* (1535), Vol. 40[I], in *D. Martin Luthers Werke*, Kritische Gesamtasgabe (Weimar Ausgabe), Vol. 40[I] (65 vols.; Weimar, Germany: Hermann Bohlaus Nachfolger, 1883ff.), 192, l.19 [hereafter referred to as WA]/ English translation in *Luther's Works*, Vol. 26 (54 vols.; St. Louis— Philadelphia: Concordia Publishing House—Fortress Press, 1955ff.), 106: "Paulos hic non agit de lana caprina nec de pane lucrando, sed de praecipuo articulo Christianae doctrinae. Illo conspecto et habito ob oculos caetera omnia vilescunt et nihili sunt. Quid enim est Petrus, Paulus, quid angelus e coelo, quid universa creatura ad ariculum iustificaitonis?" cf. ibid., WA 40[I]:48, 25/LW 26:9.

3. Reinhold Niebuhr, "Law, Conscience, and Grace" (1961), in *Justice & Mercy* (Louisville, KY: Westminster John Knox Press, 1974), 43.

4. Martin Luther, *Letter to Philip Melanchthon* (1521), in *D. Martin Luthers Werke*, Kritische Gesamtasgabe, Briefwechsel, Vol. 2 (15 vols.; Weimar, Germany: Hermann Bohlaus Nachfolger, 1930ff.), 372, l.82 [hereafter referred to as WABR]/LW48:281–82: "Si gratiae praedicator es, gratiam non fictam, sed veram praedica; si vera gratia est, verum, non fictum peccatum ferto. Deus non facit salvos ficte peccatores. Esto peccator et pecca fortiter, sed fortius fide et gaude

in Christo, qui victor est peccati, mortis et mundi. Peccandum est, quamdiu hic summus; vita haec non est habitatio iustitiae . . . ab hoc non avellet nos peccatum, etiamsi millies, millies uno die fornicemur aut occidamus. . . . Ora fortiter, etiam fortissimos peccator."

5. Martin Luther, *Evangelium am elsten Sonntag nach Trinitatis*, in *Crucigers Sommerpostille* (1543 ed.), in WA 22:210,16/*Sermons of Martin Luther*, Vol. IV, trans. and ed. John Nicholas Lenker (Grand Rapids, MI: Baker, 1988), 367: "Darumb sihe nu fort, das du auch diesem Zölner recht folgest und ym gleich werdest, Nemlich, Zum ersten, das du nicht ein falscher, sondern ein rechter Sünder seiest, das ist, nicht mit worten allein, sondern im grund und von gantzem hertzen dich fur Gott seines zorns und ewiger verdamnis schüldig erkennest, Und also mit warheit dis wort (Mir armen Sünder) fur in bringest, Aber in dem selben flugs auch das ander Wort (Sey mir gnedig) ergreiffet . . ."

6. Martin Luther, *Disputatio Heidelbergae habita* (1518), WA 1:369f, 19ff./LW 31:63: "Hoc est quod illi dicunt: Non requirit Deus perfectionem, Ubi deberent dicere: Ignoscit Deus. Sed quibus? Nunquid secures et peccatum illud non putantibus? Absit, Sed dicentibus: Dimite nobis debita nostra, ex vero corde hoc malum suum agnoscentibus et odientibus. . . . Haec est dulcisima dei Patris misericordia, quod non fictos, sed veros peccatores salvat, sustinens nos in peccatis nostris et acceptans opera et vitam nostrum omni abiectione digna, donec nos perficiat atque consummet."

7. Martin Luther, *Tischreden* (1531–1546), No. 6664, in *D. Martin Luthers Werke*, Kritische Gesamtaugabe, Tischreden, Vol. 6 (6 vols.; Weimar, Germany: Hermann Bohlaus Nachfolger, 1912–1921), 105, I.12 [hereafter referred to as WATR]: "Unser Sünden halb dass wir grosse Sünder sind, sollen wir nicht verzagen noch verzweifeln. Denn Gott, der die Vergebung der Sünden Allen, die sie von Herzen erkennen und bekennen, hat offentlich lassen verkündigen und Jdermann anbieten, Niemand ausgeschlossen, wird auch nicht anders gesinnet, sondern bleibt für und für in seinem Wort wahrhaftig und hält Glauben."

8. Martin Luther, *Evangelium am 24. Sonntag nach Trinitatis*, in *Sommerpostille 1526*, 5, 6, in WA 10$^{1/2}$: 430f., 30ff./English translation in *Sermons of Martin Luther*, V:329–30: "Fromme leut machen gehort dem Euangelio nicht zu sonder us macht nur Crysten, Es ist vil mer ein Christ sein denn fromm sein, Es kan einer wol fromm sein,

aber nicht ein Christ, Ein Christ weisst von seyner frommkeit nichts
zusagen, her findet ln im nichts gütts noch frommes, sol er fromm
sein, so müs er sich nach einer anndern un frembde frommkeit umb-
sehen… Darumb so heisst einer nicht ein Christ daher das er vil thu es
ist etwas hohers da, sonndern darumb, das er von Christo was mame,
schopffe, unnd lass im nur geben."

9. See p. 60, above.

10. Augustine, *In Epistlam Johannis ad Parthos tractatus* (c.
406/407), VII.8, in *Nicene and Post-Nicene Fathers*, ed. Philip Schaff,
First Series, Vol. 7 (reprint ed.; 2nd print.; 14 vols.; Peabody, MA:
Hendrickson, 1995), 504 [hereafter referred to as NPNF I]: "Semel
ergo breve praeceptum tibi praecipitur: Dilge, et quod vis fac: sive
taceas, dilectione taces; sive clames, dilectione clumes. . . ." For a
detailed discussion of the diversity in Augustine's thought on this
range of issues, see Mark Ellingsen, *The Richness of Augustine: His
Contextual and Pastoral Theology* (Louisville, KY: Westminster John
Knox Press, 2005), esp. 110–12.

11. Martin Luther, *Von guten Werken* (1520), WA 6:207, 4/
LW44:26–27: "Darausz dann witer floget, das einn Christen mensch,
in diessem glauben lebend, nit darff eines leres gutter werck, sondern
was ym furkumpt, das thut er, und ist alles wolgethan. . . . Das mugen
wir bey einem groben fleischlichenn exempel sehen. Wen ein man
odder weib sich zum andern vorsicht lieb und wolgefallens, und das
selb fest glemwt, wer lernet den selben, wie er sich stellen sol, was er
thun, lassen, sagen, schwigen, gedencken sol? die eynige zuvorsicht
leret yhn das alles und mehr dan not ist. Da ist yhm kein unterscheidt
in wercken. Thut das grosz, lang, vile szo gerne, als das klein, kurtz,
wenige, und widerumb, dartzu, mit frolichem, fridlichem, sicherem
hertzen und ist gantz ein frei geselle."

12. Martin Luther, *Eyn Sermon von dem heyligen hochwirdigen
Sacrament der Tauffe* (1519), WA 2:735f., 29ff./LW35:40–41.

13. Martin Luther, *Vorlesungen uber 1. Mose* (1541–1542),
WA43:532, 8/LW 5:150: "Sic in bellis sancti saepe hostes fefellerunt,
sed illa sunt mendacia, quibus licet uti in ministerio Dei adversus
Diabolum et hostes Dei."

14. Martin Luther, *Tractatus de libertate christiana* (1520), WA
7:54f., 31ff./LW 31:351–52; cf. Martin Luther, *Articuli Smalcaldici*
(1537), III.13; Luther, *In epistolam S. Pauli ad Galatas Commentarius*
(1535), WA 40^I:284.20/LW26:167–68; ibid. (1519), WA40^{II}:490,

502/ LW 27:221, 238; Martin Luther, *Resolutiones Disputationum de indulgentrium Virtute* (1518), WA 1:593, 6; 594, 25/LW31:189ff, 192; Martin Luther, *In Natali Christi* (1515), WA 1:28, 27 (teaching something like the Eastern concept of salvation as *theosis*). Cf. Augustine, *Epistulae*, CLXXXVIII (416), II.4–5/NPNF I, 1:549–50; Augustine, *Confessiones* (397/401), I.V.6; X.I.1/NPNF I, 1:46–47, 142; Augustine, *Enchiridion ad Laurentium de fide spe et caritate* (421), 31/NPNF I, 3:248. For references to the teaching of *simul iustus et peccator*, see p. 135, n.25.

For the Finnish interpretation of Luther on this matter, see Tuomo Mannermaa, *Christ Present in Faith: Luther's View of Justification*, ed. Kirsi Stjerna (Minneapolis; Fortress Press, 2005); Tuomo Mannermaa, "Why Is Luther So Fascinating? Modern Finnish Luther Research," in Carl E. Braaten and Robert W. Jenson, eds., *Union with Christ: The New Finnish Interpretation of Luther* (Grand Rapids, MI: Wm B. Eerdmans, 1998), 10–12; Simo Peuro, "Christ as Favor and Gift (donum): The Challenge of Luther's Understanding of Justification," in Braaten and Jenson, esp. 53–56. For an earlier interpreter who shared these insights about the Reformer, see Regin Prenter, *Spiritus Creator*, trans. John M. Jensen (Philadelphia: Muhlenberg Press, 1953), esp. 8, 28–29. The influence of Mysticism on Luther's commitments at this point should not be overlooked; see Reinhold Seeberg, *Die religiosen Grendgedanken des jungen Luther und ihr Verhaltnis zu dem Ockhasmismus und der deutschen Mytik* (Berlin, 1931); Heiko O. Oberman, *Luther: Man Between God and the Devil*, trans. Ellen Walliser-Scharzbart (New York: Image Books, 1992), esp. 180, 183–84; Steven Ozment, *The Age of Reform 1250–1550* (New Haven, CT: Yale University Press, 1980), 239–42. For acknowledgment of the mystical emphasis on Augustine in his treatment of grace, see J. J. O'Meara, *The Young Augustine: An Introduction to the "Confessions" of St. Augustine* (New York: Longman, 1954), esp. 203; Robert E. Wright, "Mysticism," in Alan D. Fitzgerald, ed., *Augustine through the Ages: An Encyclopedia* (Grand Rapids, MI: Wm. B. Eerdmans, 1999), 576–79.

15. Luther, *Von guten Werken*, WA 6:216, 31/LW44:38: ". . . Yn wilchem szo du sicht, das dir got szo hold ist, das er auch seinen sun fur dich gibt, musz dein hertz fusz und got widderumb hold werden . . ."

16. Luther, *In epistolomus S. Pauli ad Galatas Commenrarius* (1531/1535), WA40^{l}:433f., 26ff./LW26:277: "Et hoc viderunt omnes Prophetae, quod futurus esset omnium maximus latro, homicida,

adultery, fur sacrilegus, blasphemus, etc., quo nullus maior unquam in mundo fuerit . . ."

17. Martin Luther, *Die zweite Disputation gegen die Antinomer* (1538), WA 39^{I}:435, 18.

18. Augustine, *Confessiones*, I.IX.15/NPNF I, 1:49.

19. Albert Camus, *The Rebel: An Essay on Man in Revolt*, trans. Anthony Bower (New York: Vintage Books, 1956), 10. Much of the preceding analysis of human life is inspired by this book.

20. Ibid., 10–11, 306.

21. Luther, *Disputatio Heidelbergae habita*, 3, 19, WA 1:353f., 19ff./LW31:39, 40.

22. Martin Luther, *Vorrede aud die Epistel S. Paul an der Rome* (1546/1522), in *D. Martin Luthers Werke: Die Deutsche Bible*, Vol. 7 (9 vols.; Weimar, Germany: Hermann Bohlaus Nachfolger, 1906ff.), p.11, l. 16/LW35:370–371: "Glawb ist eyn lebendige erwegene zuuersicht auff Gottis gnade, so gewis, das er tausent mal druber sturbe, Und solch zuuersicht und erkentnis Gottlicher gnaden, macht frolich, trotzig und lustig gegen Gott, und alle Kreaturn . . ."

23. Camus, *The Rebel*, 101.

24. Ibid., 13.

25. Ibid., 304, 20.

26. Ibid., 104.

27. Luther, *Vorrede aud die Epistel S. Paul an der Rome*, in *D. Martin Luthers Werke: Die Deutsche Bible*, Vol. 7, 11, l. 6/LW35:370–371.

28. Luther, *Tischreden* (1531), 124, WATR 1:52, 29: "Vult Deus, ut simus laeti, et odit tristitiam. Si enim vellet nos tristes esse, non daret solem, lunam et alios fructus terrae, quos omnes dat ad laetitiam. Faceret tenebras. Non sineret amplius oriri solem aut redire aestatem."

29. Martin Luther, *Ein Quidecim Psalmos Graddum* (1532/1533), WA40^{III}196, 11.

30. Martin Luther, *Vorlesing uber Iesaia* (1527–1529), WA 25:347, 16: "Possumus autem ex gaudio intelligere defectum fidei nostrae: quantum enim credimus, tantum necesse et gaudere."

31. Martin Luther, *Die Vorlesung uber den Romerbrief* (1515–1516), WA56:465,1ff./LW25:457; WA56:423,23ff./LW25:415; Martin Luther, *Dictata super Psalterium* (1513–1515), WA4:360,6ff/LW11:490.

32. Martin Luther, *Vorlesung uber der Prediger Solomo* (1526), WA20:38, 16/LW15:31–32.

33. Luther, *Tischreden* (1531), No. 122. WATR 1:49f., 27/
LW54:17–18: "Experientia doctus possum docere, quomodo in ten-
tationibus instituere animum debeos. Quando tentaris tristitia aut
desperatione aut alio dolore conscientiae, tunc ede, bibe, quaere col-
loquia; si potes de cogitatione puellae recreare, facito."

34. Luther, *Tractatus de libertate christiana* (1520), WA 7:53, 15/
LW31:349: "Cum autem haec promissa dei sint verba sancta, vera,
iusta, libera, pacata et universa bonitate plena, fit, ut anima, quae
firma fide illis adheret, sic eis uniatur, immo penitus absorbeatur, ut
non modo participet sed saturetur et inebrietur omni virtute eorum."

35. Martin Luther, *Das XIV. Und XV. Kapitel S.* Johannis (1537–
1538), WA45:671, 25/LW 24:230.

36. Luther, *Tishcreden* (1532), 1822, WATR 2:229, 12: "Ich solt
so frolich sein, das ich vor freuden solt gantz gesundt sein und solt
nicht konnen kranckh werden vor freuden."

CHAPTER 5
Brave Sinning Makes for a Joyful Life!

1. Among books seeking to relate cutting-edge neurobiology to
theology are Andrew Newberg and Mark Robert Waldman, *Why We
Believe What We Believe: Uncovering Our Biological Need for Meaning,
Spirituality, and Truth* (New York: Free Press, 2006); Andrew B.
Newberg, Vince Rause, and Eugene D'Aquili, *Why God Won't Go
Away: Brain Science and the Biology of Belief* (New York: Ballantine
Books, 2002); Eugene D'Aquili and Andrew Newberg, *The Mystical
Mind: Probing the Biology of Religious Experience* (Minneapolis: Fortress
Press, 1999); Dean Hamer, *The God Gene: How Faith Is Hardwired
into Our Genes* (New York: Arbour Books, 2004); Rhawn Joseph, *The
Transmitter to God* (Berkeley: University Press of California, 2001);
Gregory R. Peterson, *Minding God: Theology and the Cognitive Sciences*
(Minneapolis: Fortress Press, 2003); David A. Hogue, *Remembering
the Future, Imagining the Past: Story, Ritual, and the Human Brain*
(Cleveland: The Pilgrim Press, 2003); James B. Ashbrook, *The Human
Mind and the Mind of God: Theological Promise in Brain Research*
(Lanham, MD: University Press of America, 1984); Kelly Bulkeley,
ed., *Soul, Psyche, Brain: New Directions in the Study of Religion and
Brian-Mind Science* (New York: Palgrave Macmillan, 2005); Mario

Beauregard and Denyse O'Leary, *The Spiritual Brain: A Neuroscientist's Case for the Existence of the Soul* (New York: Harper One, 2007); Kevin S. Seybold, *Explorations in Neuroscience, Psychology and Religion* (Burlington, VT: Ashgate, 2007); Michael R. Trimble, *The Soul in the Brain: The Basics of Language, Art, and Belief* (Baltimore: Johns Hopkins University Press, 207), esp. 159–75. None of these volumes take into account the implications of monoamines for the doctrines of Sin and Sanctification as I have.

2. For this description of the human brain I am indebted to David Kahn, "From Chaos to Self-Organization: The Brain, Dreaming, and Religious Experience," in Bulkeley, *Soul, Psyche, Brain*, 139ff.

3. Newberg, Rause, and D'Aquili, *Why God Won't Go Away*; Richard Davidson, J. Kabat-Zinn, J. Shumacher, M. Rosenkranz, D. Muller, S. Santonelli, F. Ubanowski, A. Harrington, K. Bonus, and J. Sheridan, "Alterations in brain and immune function produced by mindfulness meditation," *Psychosomatic Medicine* 65 (2003): 564–70; also see Hamer, *The God Gene*, 121–23.

4. Hamer, *The God Gene*, 122. On the executive function of the brain's frontal lobe, see Elkhonon Goldberg, *The Executive Brain: Frontal Lobes and the Civilized Mind* (New York: Oxford University Press, 2002).

5. Hamer, *The God Gene*, 123; Newberg, Rause, and D'Aquili, *Why God Won't Go Away*.

6. Hamer, *The God Gene*, 104–5.

7. Ibid., 105; Andrew B. Newberg and J. Iverson, "The neural basis of the complex mental task of meditation: neurotransmitter and neurochemical considerations," *Medical Hypotheses* 61, no. 2 (2003): 288. Daniel G. Amen, *Change Your Brain, Change Your Life* (New York: Three Rivers Press, 1998), 93.

8. Hamer, *The God Gene*, 72ff.

9. Ibid., 70–76, 116–17, 138–39. For more on the role of VMAT2, see Max V. Myakishev et al., "High Throughput SNP Genotyping by Allel Specific PCR with Universal Energy-Transfer-Labeled Primers," *Genome Research* 11 (2001): 163–69; George Uhl et al., "The VMAT2 Gene in Mice and Humans: Amphetamine Responses, Locomotion, Cardiac Arrhythmias, Aging, and Vulnerability to Dopaminergic Toxins," *The FASB Journal* 14 (2000): 2459–65.

10. Beauregard and O'Leary, *The Spiritual Brain*, 51–55; Carl Zimmer, "Faith-Boosting Genes: A Search for the Genetic Basis of Spirituality," *Scientific American* (September 27, 2004).

11. Beauregard and O'Leary, *The Spiritual Brain*, 259–60, 263ff. Activation of the parietal region along with the lateral prefrontal region in brains engaging in meditation was found by S. W. Lazar et al., "Functional brain mapping of the relaxation response and meditation," *NeuroReport* 11 (2000): 1581–85.

12. Beauregard and O'Leary, *The Spiritual Brain*, 273; Newberg and Iverson, "The neural basis of the complex mental task of meditation," 285ff. Also see J. Cornwall and O. T. Phillipson, "Mediodorsal and reticular thalamic nuclei receive collateral axons from prefrontal cortex and laterodorsal tegmental nucleus in the rat," *Neurosci Lett* 88 (1988): 121–26; D. J. Bucci, M. Conley, and M. Gallagher, "Thalmic and basal forebrain cholinergic connections of the rat posterior parietal cortex," *NeuroReport* 10 (1999): 941–45.

13. For this exposition of the new insights in neurobiological research, I am indebted to Stefan Klein, *The Science of Happiness: How Our Bodies Make Us Happy—and What We Can Do to Get Happier* (New York: Marlowe & Company, 2006), 35–37, 56–58, 107; also Michael Lemonick, "The Biology of Joy," *Time* 17 (January 17, 2005), A12–A19; Hamer, *The God Gene*, esp. 103–8.

14. See R. E. Wheeler, R. J. Davidson, and A. J. Tomarken, "Frontal Brain Asymmetry and Emotional Reactivity: A Biological Substrate of Affective State," *Psychophysiologie* 30 (1993): 547–58.

15. Giovanni Fava, "Well-Being Therapy: Conceptual and Technical Issues," *Psychotherapy and Psychosomatics* 68 (1999): 171–79; Klein, *The Science of Happiness*, 202–4. New books describing how spirituality (exercise of the left prefrontal cortex) also exercises brain circuits enhancing feelings of joy and happiness include Sharon Begley, *Train Your Mind, Change Your Brain: How a New Science Reveals Our Extraordinary Potential to Transform Ourselves* (New York: Ballantine Books, 2007); Norman Doidge, *The Brain That Changes Itself: Stories of Personal Triumph for the Frontiers of Brain Science* (New York: Viking Press, 2007). For books on how gratitude (a byproduct of God-centeredness) enhances happiness, see Robert Emmons, *Thanks! How the New Science of Gratitude Can Make You Happier* (Boston: Houghton Mifflin, 2007).

16. Joseph Carroll, "Most Americans 'Very Satisfied' with Their Personal Lives," 2007, at www.gallup.com/poll/103483/Most-Americans-Very-Satisfied-Their-Personal [accessed November 24, 2008]. The ratio of happiness among frequent churchgoers is even higher according to the Pew Research Center, "Are We Happy Yet?" posted February

13, 2006, http://pewresearch.org/pubs/302/are-we-happy-yet [accessed January 1, 2008]. National Opinion Research Center, General Social Survey (2004), as reported in Arthur G. Brooks, "Why We're Happy," *Readers' Digest* (July 2008), 166.

17. Wheeler et al., "Frontal Brain Asymmetry," 547–58; cf. N. Adler, "Stress and Health: Biology, Behaviour, and the Social Environment" (lecture presented at the Annual Conference of the American Association for the Advancement of Science, San Francisco, 2001); Klein, *The Science of Happiness*, esp. 239. On religion's positive impact on health, also see Harold G. Koenig, Michael E. McCullogh, and David B. Lawson, *Handbook of Religion and Health* (Oxford: Oxford University Press, 2001); Peter C. Hill and Eric M. Butler, "The role of religion in promoting physical health," *Journal of Psychology and Christianity* 14 (1995): 141–55.

18. David Brinn, "Israeli researchers discover gene for altruism," in *Our Jerusalem*, posted January 23, 2005, http://www.ourjerusalem.com/news/story/news20050124.html [accessed December 28, 2007], reporting on research by Richard Ebstein, *Modern Psychiatry* (January 2005).

19. Laura Smart Richman, Laura Kubzansky, et al., "Positive Emotion and Health: Going Beyond the Negative," *Health Psychology* 24, no. 4 (1999): 422–29. Also reported in Lemonick, "The Biology of Joy," A17. On dopamine's role in contributing to hopefulness, see Jerome Groopman, "The Anatomy of Hope," *The Permanente Journal* (Spring 2004), at http://xnet.kp.org/permanentejournal/Spring04/com [accessed January 8, 2008].

20. Robert A. Emmons and Michael E. McCullough, "Highlights from the Research Project on Gratitude" (n.d.), at http://psychology.ucdavis.edu/labs/emmons [accessed Jan. 7, 2008]; Emmons, *Thanks!* Also reported in Lemonick, "The Biology of Joy," A17.

21. For this construal by Luther, see pp. 70–71. For the role of dopamine in heterosexual attractions, see Helen Fisher, *The Anatomy of Love: A Natural History of Mating, Marriage, and Why We Stray* (New York: Random House, 1994); Larry J. Young and Zuoxin Wang, "The neurobiology of pair bonding," *Nature Neuroscience* 7 (September 26, 2004).

22. Kerstin Uvnas-Moberg, *The Oxytocin Factor: Tapping the Hormone of Calm, Love, and Healing*, trans. Roberta Francis (Cambridge, MA: Merloyd Lawrence Books, 2003).

CHAPTER 6
How Brave Sinning Could Change American Life

1. International Labour Organization, Sept. 2, 2007, at www.ilo.org/global/About_the_ILO/Media [accessed May 14, 2008]; U.S. Census Bureau report, "Labor Day 2008," at http://www.census.gov/Press-Release [accessed November 27, 2008]. The National Sleep Foundation 2008 report can be accessed at http://www.sleepfoundation.org/site.

2. "Annual Expedia Survey Reveals Nearly One of Every Three American Workers Are Vacation Deprived," April 15, 2008, at http://press.expedia.com/index [accessed May 14, 2008].

3. Gallup Poll, "Most Americans 'Very Satisfied' With Their Personal Lives" (December 31, 2007) (at http://gallup.com/poll/103483/Most-Americans-Very-Satisfied [accessed November 27, 2008]); Gallup Poll, "More Than Half of Americans 'Very Satisfied' With Personal Life" (January 3, 2007) (at http://www.gallup.com/poll/26032/Most-Americans [accessed November 27, 2008].

4. For these statistics, see John Fetto, "What Seems to Be the Problem?" in *American Demographics*, April 1, 2002, at http://findarticles.com/p/articles/mi_m4021/is_ai_87109755 [accessed November 26, 2008].

5. Bureau of Justice Statistics, "Drug use" (2007), at http://www.ojp.usdoj.gov/bjs/dcf/du.htm [accessed November 27, 2008].

6. For these statistics, see R. A. Cohen, "Health Insurance Coverage: Early Release of Estimates from the National Health Interview Survey, 2007," National Center for Health Statistics, June 25, 2008; summary available at http://www.cdc.gov/nchs/pressroom/08newsreleases/uninsured.htm [accessed December 1, 2008].

7. See Dan Hamilton, "Rich-Poor Gap Widens in Europe, North America" (2008), at http://newsweek.washingtonpost.com/postglobal/sais/nexteurope/2008/10 [accessed November 27, 2008].

8. The Harris Poll #24 (May 3, 2000), at http://www.harrisinteractive.com/harris_poll/index.asp [accessed November 27, 2008].

9. Center for American Progress, "Understanding Mobility in America," April 26, 2006, at http://www.americanprogress.org/issues/2006/04/b1579981.html [accessed November 27, 2008].

10. For specifics of this critique, see Mark Ellingsen, *When Did Jesus Become Republican? Rescuing Our Country and Our Values from the Right* (New York: Rowman & Littlefield, 2007), 57–89.

11. Rick Warren, *The Purpose Driven Life: What On Earth Am I Here For?* (Grand Rapids, MI: Zondervan, 2002), 117–67, 283–84 (see also pp. 127–128, nn.58–60).

12. For this analysis I am indebted to Richard Sennett, *The Corrosion of Character: The Personal Consequences of Work in the New Capitalism* (New York: W. W. Norton & Co., 1998), 146–47.

13. Ibid., 116.

14. Martin Luther, *De zwite Disputation gegen die Antinomer* (1538), in *D. Martin Luthers Werke*, Kritische Gesamtausgabe (Weimar Ausgabe), Vol.39¹ (65 vols.; Weimar, Germany: Hermann Bohlaus Nachfolger, 1883ff.), 435, l.18 [hereafter referred to as WA]: "Caeterum nostra lex vacua cesset per Christum, qui replete vacuitatem illam, primum per sesse extra nos, quia ipsemet implet legem pro nobi, deinde replete etiam per Spiritum sanctum in nobis . . ."

15. Andrew Newberg, Eugene D'Aquili, and Vance Rause, *Why God Won't Go Away: Brain Science and the Biology of Belief* (New York: Ballantine, 2001).

16. For this analysis I am indebted to Dean Hamer, *The God Gene: How Faith Is Hardwired into Our Genes* (New York: Anchor Books, 2004), esp. 143.

17. Richard Dawkins, *The Selfish Gene* (New York: Oxford University Press, 1976).

18. Augustine, *De civitate Dei* (413–26), II.4; XIV.28, in *Nicene and Post-Nicene Fathers*, ed. Philip Schaff, First Series, Vol. 2 (reprint ed.; 2nd print.; 14 vols.; Peabody, MA: Hendrickson, 1995), 24–25, 282–83 (hereafter referred to as NPNF I); Martin Luther, *Auslegung des 101. Psalms* (1534–1535), WA51:242ff., 21ff./English translation in *Luther's Works*, Vol. 13, ed. Jaroslav Pelikan and Helmut Lehmann (54 vols.; Philadelphia and St. Louis: Fortress Press and Concordia Publishing House, 1955–1974), 198–99 [hereafter referred to as LW]; Martin Luther, *Uon welltlicher uberkeytt wie weytt man yhr gehorsam schuldig sey* (1523), WA 11; 251–52/ LW 45:91–92.

19. Augustine, *De civitate Dei* (413–426), XIX.11, 13–17; XVIII.2/NPNF I 2:407, 409–13, 399.

20. Reinhold Niebuhr, "We See Through a Glass Darkly' (1960), in *Justice & Mercy*, ed. Ursula Niebuhr (Louisville, KY: Westminster John Knox Press, 1974), 36; Martin Luther, *Evangelium an dreiundzwanzigsten Sonntag nach Trinitatis*, 19, in *Sommerpostille 1526*, WA

10: 424f., 37 / English translation in *The Complete Sermons of Martin Luther*, Vol. III.1, ed. John N. Lenker (Grand Rapids, MI: Baker Books, 2000), 302–3.

21. Reinhold Niebuhr, *Moral Man and Immoral Society* (New York: Charles Scribner's Sons, 1932), 231–56.

22. To get a flavor for the progressive sociopolitical positions of these denominations, see Mark Ellingsen, *The Cutting Edge: How Churches Speak on Social Issues* (Geneva: WCC Publications, 1993). For an analysis of the failure of these churches and theologians to make a difference in the American politics of today, see Ellingsen, *When Did Jesus Become Republican?*

23. James Madison, "No. 10," in *The Federalist Papers* (New York: Mentor, 1961), 78; James Madison, *Notes of Debates in the Federal Convention of 1787, Reported by James Madison* (New York: Library of America, 1987), 52, 131.

24. James Madison, "No. 38," in *The Federalist Papers*, 230; Alexander Hamilton, "No. 85," in *The Federalist Papers*, 523–24.

25. James Madison, "Parties" (1792), in *The Papers of James Madison, 1791–1793*, Vol. 14 (Charlottesville: University Press of Virginia, 1983), 197.

26. Alexander Hamilton, "No. 36," in *The Federalist Papers*, 222–23.

27. Augustine, *Confessiones* (399), I.9.15/NPNF I 1:49.

28. Martin Luther, *Tractatus de libertate christiana* (1520), WA7:53, 15/LW 31:349.

29. Martin Luther, *Das XIV und XV Kapitel S. Johannis* (1537–1538), WA45:25, 25/LW24: 230: "Den ein solcher mensch, was er lebt und thut, es sey gros oder gering und heisse, wie es wolle, so sind es eitel fruchte nicht sein. . . . Und wird einem solchem alles, so er thut, leicht und on saure erbeit oder verdies, ist ym nichts zu schwer oder zu gros, das er nicht leiden und tragen konne. . . ."

30. See pp. 81–94, for details and documentation.

31. Martin Luther, *Epistel S. Petri gepredigt und ausgelegt* (1522), WA12:333, 12/LW 30:78–79: "Sonst wo es jemand von myr begeret, dem ich damit dienen kunde, will ichs gerne von güttem willen thun Also sollen nu alle unsere werck seyn, das sie aufs lust und lieb daher fliessen, und alle gegen dem nehisten gericht seyn, weyl myr fur uns selbs nicht durffen, das wyr frum werden."

CONCLUSION

1. Martin Luther, *Epistel am Ostermittwoch*, in *Crucigers Sommerpostille* (1544), in *D. Martin Luthers Werke*, Kritische Gesamtausgabe (Weimar Ausgabe), Vol. 21 (65 vols.; Weimar, Germany: Hermann Bohlaus Nachfolger, 1883ff.), 273, l.24 [hereafter referred to as WA]/English translation in *The Complete Sermons of Martin Luther*, Vol. IV.1, ed. John Nicholas Lenker (Grand Rapids, MI: Baker Books, 2000), 227–28; Martin Luther, *Adnotationes Quincuplici Psalterio adscriptae* (1513), WA 4:476, 26ff.

2. See Martin Luther, *Letter to Philip Melanchthon* (1521), in *D. Martin Luthers Werke*, Kritische Gesamtausgabe, Briefwechsel, Vol. 2 (15 vols.; Weimar, Germany: Hermann Bohlaus Nachfolger, 1930ff.), 372, l.82/LW48:281–82: "Si gratiae praedicator es, gratiam non fictam, sed veram praedica; si vera gratia est, verum, non fictum peccatum ferto. Deus non facit salvos ficte peccatores. Esto peccator et pecca fortiter, sed fortius fide et gaude in Christo, qui victor est peccati, mortis et mundi. Peccandum est, quamdiu hic summus; vita haec non est habitatio iustitiae . . . ab hoc non avellet nos peccatum, etiamsi millies, millies uno die fornicemur aut occidamus. . . . Ora fortiter, etiam fortissimos peccator."